IT TAKES
5YEARS
TO BECOME A
TEACHER

ROS WILSON
WITH **KIRSTIE PILMER**

IT TAKES **5 YEARS** TO BECOME A **TEACHER**
Written by Ros Wilson with Kirstie Pilmer
Edited and Proof Read by Richard Robinson
Cover and Design by Dan Wilson

Published by P and R Education Ltd.
83 Haigh Lane, Haigh, Wakefield, West Yorkshire, S75 4DA.

www.RosWilsonEd.com
hello@RosWilsonEd.com
Twitter: @RosBigWriting

ISBN: 978-1-8381761-0-5

First Published in 2020. First Edition.

CONTENTS

FOREWORD

Dame Alison Peacock

On Pond Dipping During Final PGCE Placement

What I had not realised was that when the nets scraped along the bottom of the pond some of what was collected was mud. Within the mud, it transpired, there were small, black, slimy leeches. During the hour of lunch, some of these leeches in the buckets had edged their way up the sides of each container...

Later, having transported the pond contents back to the pond, Dame Alison was driving home having successfully completed her final placement:

Little did I realise that a particularly persistent leech was making its way up the back of my driving seat, heading with determination towards the skin on my neck...

The remainder of my teaching career has continued in the same vein. Many joyful times, full of hard work, risk-taking and laughter; with the occasional 'leech on the back of your neck' moment.

Good luck as you join our wonderful profession and pursue the best job in the world.

FOREWORD

Professor Sam Twiselton OBE

Why We Are Proud to Be Teachers

I ask them why their job gets them up in the morning. I nearly always find we basically share the same thoughts; on a good day – a day when it's not just about paying the mortgage or catching up on gossip – I'm talking about the days when we know we're doing something important, that matters, that makes a difference.

The words and phrases about why I love my job that pop into my mind include just that – it is about making a difference, but also the why and the how? It is because we all know that ultimately education in all its forms has the power to transform lives, open gateways, change individuals, the communities they live in, society, the world! Without education we would not have any of the other things our civilised lives depend on.

INTRODUCTION

It Takes Five Years...

It takes five years in the classroom to become a confident and fully competent teacher. We all struggled in the beginning. No one should feel they are not going to make it because they walk out of university and into the classroom feeling they know very little about the craft of teaching.

As you read about the struggles and challenges so many of us met, be assured that every one of us persevered and that throughout our stories there runs a common thread of pride in our profession and gratitude for the support and advice we received on our journeys. We are all proud and pleased to be teachers!

I am particularly moved and proud of the contributions to this publication from friends and colleagues across the spectrum of the profession. They have told their diverse stories with a deep sincerity and respect for all, and often with humour, yet there are common threads throughout that show a consistency and commitment that makes our profession one of the greatest in the world.

Thank you all:
(By alphabetical order of surname)

Rachel Colbourn
Headteacher, Bramhope Primary School, Leeds

Chris Dyson
Headteacher, Parklands Primary School, Leeds

Dr Emma Kell
Education Consultant, trainer of teachers, writer and speaker

Sarah Mullin
Deputy Headteacher, Priory School, Edgbaston

Dame Alison Peacock
Chief Executive of the Chartered College of Teaching

Halil Tamgumus
Headteacher, Braunstone Community Primary School, Leicester

Professor Sam Twiselton OBE
Director, Sheffield Institute of Education

With **Kirstie Pilmer**
Class teacher in her fifth year in the profession

With acknowledgements to the generous writers of the case studies in *Chapter 16:*

- Sara Alston
- Humaira Batool
- Ginny Bootman
- Alex Caunt
- Sharon Day
- Joshua Denton-Collins
- Rachel Gregson
- Sam Keys
- Steve Ladd
- Hayley McDonnell
- Katy McCullough
- Tamsin Nellist
- Audrey Pantelis
- Debbie Rainer
- David Rushby
- Jen Reynolds
- Stephen Rogers
- Terry Ross

RACHEL COLBOURN

Welcome to the Profession

My final days of teaching practice felt like a dream. It was summertime in rural Lincolnshire. I was in an idyllic village school of 60 pupils where I knew every child. I had a first-class honours degree in the bag and had already signed up for a master's degree the following year. As I neared the end of my placement, the headteacher had offered to pay me to teach for the rest of the summer term and, out of 600 aspiring applicants, I was one of the lucky 40 who were chosen to take up a position within the London Borough of Kensington and Chelsea from the following September.

Fast forward three months and I was sitting in a staffroom in Eltham, 13 miles and a million light years from Kensington. The position I had been expecting had not come to fruition; I needed to get a job and start paying off my student debt and, to be honest, I would have taken pretty much anything.

I was one of three NQTs appointed at Eltham. There was not so much an induction as a series of warnings. There was no point planning as we could just use last year's worksheets. Communication with parents was not just discouraged, it was dangerous. We were not able to access the site after school hours (it was only a year after the murder of Stephen Lawrence, the 18 year old who was stabbed to death by a gang of white youths as he waited at the local bus stop) and, the deputy told me, if I was finding things hard, I was to remember that 'the little sh*ts were paying for our new telly...'

The following year was an exhausted blur of forgotten conversations across a smoke-filled staffroom. There were lots of headlice and plenty of fights; fights between the children, fights with the professionals (what was I expected to do with Oliver when he wouldn't do anything I asked of him?) and fights with my mentor to provide something better than the seemingly endless cloze procedure worksheets which hung around the 'Viking' topic like a bad smell.

There were some stand out moments too: cowering under the desk because an angry parent had appeared on site threatening to shoot me and having to be escorted home for my own protection. Hearing (then seeing) the headteacher pull a boy by his hair down the entire length of the corridor. Finding out that my permanent contract was, in fact, only temporary... It was not really what I had envisaged for my first year in teaching and there were many times when I wondered if I had made a mistake. I felt as though I could put nothing I had learned into practice; that I had been a fraud throughout my years at teacher training college and that I was, for the most part, a failure.

Sometimes I meet new teachers who are also feeling like this. Hang in there, I tell them. Try these strategies, look at what you have achieved, let me help you make a plan for this coming year and, above all, do not be afraid to move schools. More on this in a minute.

'Why did you go into teaching?' is a question every NQT is asked at interview. 'Why stay in teaching?' is much more difficult to answer. There are not many jobs where the contracted hours equate to roughly half of your working week, where you feel ill with the all-consuming responsibility for each and every day and where you never, ever feel you have done enough. But there are also not many jobs where you are in the privileged position of shaping our nation's future; where you are brought to tears with the difference you have been able to make; and where, in years to come, a parent will come and thank you and tell you that you will never understand what you did for their child.

There are no shortcuts to learning on the job. Now that I have been in education for 27 years, I know that however hard it felt at the time, I have learned from all eight of the schools I have worked in. Teaching should take you out of your comfort zone and challenge you. If it does not, it might be time to move on, but not before you have a) stuck it out a bit and b) tried a different school.

It was not until I worked in Malaysia, five years after I had qualified, that I realised how cultural our education system really is. Of course, it is obvious when you think about it, but working alongside Malaysian staff, as well as those from Australia and New Zealand, profoundly challenged what I had always thought of as 'normal'. What is so special about sitting nicely on the carpet or being able to stand in a line? That is the joy of being a new teacher, having the capacity to (sensitively and maybe not immediately) challenge some of the status quo that you will find in every school. Headteachers appoint new teachers because they seek change, so don't be afraid to voice your opinions and ideas, right from the start.

It was not until I worked in a school with alarmingly high levels of deprivation and complex needs, that I really understood what was meant by a personalised curriculum. Working at a school in York, where behaviour management became a fundamental part of every day, rather than a set of theoretical principles, challenged my communication skills even after 13 years in the profession. The insistence of some children I was teaching that they were never going to do any work forced me to have new conversations as a means of motivating and engaging children who refused to be motivated and engaged.

From 2000-2009, I lived and worked in Oman in the Middle East. It was there that I really began to understand inclusivity, diversity and the complexity of what it meant to be 'British'. With 56 nationalities and many second-generation expats, it was important to define who you were and where you came from. Working without access to a local authority also gave me a confidence to think things through for myself – vital when you come into a profession tightly bound in statutory guidance, school policies and with a mind-boggling array of seemingly endless well-meaning advice. When something went wrong, it was not a case of 'what usually happens in this circumstance' but what should I do in this case (and why) – something which has stayed with me to this day.

The six years I spent working in a private school in Harrogate again challenged some of my own prejudices and allowed me to see for myself what you are actually able to offer over and above when you are in a 'bubble' of 15 – something we have all become familiar with in the pandemic conditions of 2020.

The point is, I have never stopped learning. In fact, the longer I have taught, the more I have realised how much more I have to learn about what makes good teaching. Of course, there are some underlying, fundamental truths about education, whatever the context. In recent years, my visits to our sister school in Uganda have particularly highlighted the fact that, whatever their socio-economic background or life experience, children generally want to learn and parents generally want the best for their child. Simple, eh?

It is a long time since I started at Eltham, but every time I appoint a teacher in their first years of teaching, I feel the responsibility of helping one more teacher embark on their career. This year is no exception. The NQT I have appointed has visited our school twice, but I have not even seen her teach. What she does have is an outstanding track record, great references, a first-class degree and a desire to do her very best. Sounds familiar, I know.

The quest to do our best for children is never easy but it is something I have striven to do wherever and whoever I have taught. It will often mean more work, may occasionally make you unpopular and will involve an awful lot of thinking. My advice to all new teachers and especially those from the 2020 cohort is do not panic if teaching is not what you initially expected, seek out new teaching experiences throughout your career, and make a commitment to learn from each and every one of them. It is an exciting time to be joining the profession. We are seeking thoughtful, reflective practitioners and we look forward to your arrival.

Rachel Colbourn
Headteacher, Bramhope Primary School, Leeds

CHRIS DYSON

Sharing the Love

I came to Parklands Primary School as headteacher six years ago. At the time I took over the headship, the school was classified as inadequate, standards were at rock bottom, 150 pupils were excluded and both a padded cell and an isolation room were in full use. Prior to my starting, there were around 20 children who daily went on the roof 'for fun'. Staff mobility was very high and the fact that the school had seen five different heads in 2013/14 meant staff morale was extremely low. Being expected to repeatedly change, and adopt five different philosophies and ways of doing things in one year, really affected staff morale and school life.

Fast forward six years and the difference is there for all to see. The school is Ofsted rated 'Outstanding' and has been in the top 1% of schools for the past four years in maths and the top 5% in reading and writing. Staff morale is exceptionally high with 22 teaching staff having only 21 days of sick leave last year between them, and staff turnover is drastically reduced with us seeing only three people leave in six years (all for promotion). Exclusions dropped to one in six years and nobody goes on the roof anymore. The padded cell has been ripped out and the exclusion room turned into a music room to celebrate the arts.

So how did this transformation come about? It was turned around by using a carrot and not a stick approach. It was brought about by putting the wellbeing of staff and children at the very heart of everything we do.

When I was a teaching deputy head, my daughter got the title role of Upsy Daisy Angel in her Reception Christmas production. Being Reception, the only shows were at 11am and 1pm. I asked to attend and my headteacher replied:

'Who will teach your class?'
So, sadly, I missed her starring moment.

My son has a real dislike of school but he excelled at sport. To my sorrow, I was never allowed to watch him race at sports day, play for the school football and cricket teams or take part in any of the other things he was great at. So, when I became a head, I told my staff that if they ever needed to see their child in their own school they could just go and I (or my deputy head) would have their class. This type of response immediately gets an extra 10% from staff.

When I was 24 and at the start of my teaching career, my house mate was getting married. Not being a teacher, he was getting married on a Friday. I had a head who might have said yes I could go (I was an usher) but equally they could have said no. So, not being able to miss my best mate's wedding, I took a 'sick day' and then to make it more realistic, I took three days sick leave! I didn't want my staff being put in the same position so, upon becoming headteacher, I offered lieu days to staff in exchange for in-service days attended in their own time.

These lieu days can be added up over two years meaning all staff could bank ten days in lieu. The result of these actions saw staff sick leave drop from 234 days to 21 as teachers could book time to do whatever they fancied. Having a young staff, there are lots of 'hen' and 'stag' dos to attend but our staff can now book them off on full pay as opposed to playing the sick card. The impact of positive staff wellbeing brings smiles, confidence and trust. If staff are not off ill, they are in class every day and the children have consistency, which brings higher standards and maintains excellent behaviour.

Putting the child at the centre of everything brings respect and a love of the school. We play music 24/7 and we make school a happy, safe place to be. Attendance has risen from 88% in 2013/14 to 97% in 2020. On Fridays, attendance for the last four years is at 99.7% as simply nobody wants to miss #FundayFriday at the #FunPalace as we celebrate, with over 140 parents attending, our #bestseatsinthehouse assembly.

Having fun doesn't mean a lowering of standards, in 2018 we recorded the highest maths progress score in the country. 78% of children gained greater depth in maths, with progress being at the world record score of +9.0. These figures will never be beaten. How did we do it? By having happy, motivated, trusted teachers. I made a point at Parklands of treating everybody as an equal. The teachers, teaching assistants, office staff, lunch time staff – everyone. When we team bond, we team bond as a unit, excluding nobody.

I explained to staff we are lifelong learners; we will all make mistakes – it is how you deal with the mistakes that matters. My office door is never closed. If a member of staff wishes to talk with me, they just come in – no appointment needed and no judgment made. Trust is key – and realising everyone has a talent.

My biggest problems as a newly qualified teacher were both associated with myself rather than with the children. I loved teaching right from the start – I knew I would. I never expected any problems with discipline or rudeness and I rarely had any. I would laugh at children if they tried to get out of line, but then – of course – I was a tall, well-built man and a large personality... built to teach!

I started teaching before the days of Ofsted and rigorous accountability and basically, I did what I wanted, and no one seemed to try to make me do differently. My class and I spent the mornings on times tables, maths and news and every afternoon without fail (as long as it was dry) we went out to play cricket. The children loved it and we had so much fun.

So, what were my problems?

My first problem was arrogance. I thought I knew it all and I let that be known from my first days in school. This really annoyed many of the staff and I can fully understand why now. I must have been so irritating. Besides, I didn't know it all – obviously. But if you believe you know it all, you don't seek advice and you don't listen to advice when it is offered. Now, as a head, I expect our young staff to listen to advice and we give them plenty. I must have been quite hard to manage all those years ago.

My second problem was women.

I think I will stop there!

What a time to start in the greatest profession in the world. Three months ago, as we entered March 2020, the final year graduates were preparing for the end of their courses, the courses which they had worked so hard in for the past few years... then, from nowhere, we had lockdown. No final placements, no graduating with the people you had shared your journeys with... just confusion.

When September starts, so will so many new careers and quite simply the education priorities will need to be changed. At least you won't be starting by preparing children for the 'test' season.

Currently we test/assess in:
- Reception Baseline then the Foundation Stage Profile
- Year 1 - Phonics Check
- Year 2 - Phonics Re-sits and SATs
- Year 4 - Times Table Checking Exercise
- Year 6 - SATs

That is five exams in the first seven years of school for very young children!

In September, the new graduate's role will be about empathy, wellbeing and trying to answer the question, 'What on earth just happened?' We will see affluent families who have seen their jobs 'disappear', we will see the world in deep recession, we will see anxiety in children that we have never seen before. So, my advice is smile, be confident and be receptive as you are the key to these children's lives. They will need understanding and love, they won't need 'cramming' for exams!

The key for new teachers is to showcase your skills, whether it is times tables, a love of reading, a love of writing, art, music, historical knowledge, anything... showcase to the headteacher and share with colleagues. Being an NQT doesn't mean you are not as good as the established teachers; it just means you have less experience.

Smile every day and love the children, love the community and respect every member of staff in the team. Teaching is the greatest job in the world. If you have a dark day, talk about it – we have all had them.

Be confident from the day you walk into school as it will be a totally new educational world where nobody is more experienced than anyone else. You will be starting your career as a new light and new hope, and feel free to contact me at any time for guidance and support.

Chris Dyson
Headteacher, Parklands Primary School, Leeds

DR EMMA KELL

Snot in the Office and German Magazines

Lessons from My Early Years in Teaching

It's 1999. Pulp provides our anthem. My friends and I do meet up as the gongs ring for 2000. We even find a fountain and some cheap cider for old time's sake, but it all feels a little odd. We've scattered to different parts of the country, living on meagre salaries in new and disconcerting contexts, experimenting with 'adulthood' but still feeling very much like children.

I'm an NQT. I'm straight out of university. Bright-eyed, optimistic, naïve and raring to change the world. Newly single, I'm flat sharing and looking forward to new networks of friends. The school is a rural one – the pub culture I'd anticipated doesn't really exist. At the end of a Friday, people drive miles to their families and homes. I haven't yet learned the importance of reaching out and asking for help. I'm lonely and struggling. A 'good girl' at school and university, the daily affirmations are harder to find. I'm conditioned to give the appearance of having everything completely under control when in fact I don't have a clue. My students regard me with wry amusement – never hostility. They listen occasionally but not a lot. Young people are very perceptive. They are kind – indulgent even – they know I'm floundering.

'No Good to Anyone'

A few months in, I call a teacher helpline. 'I can't eat; I can't sleep; I've got no energy for friends or family,' I say. 'Well you're no good to anyone then,' says the person at the other end of the line. Harsh words (and ones that probably wouldn't be used today) but actually, the jolt I need. They led to one of my ongoing mantras: 'You can't teach well if you're a worn-out husk'.

No point waiting for someone else to come and bail me out of the ridiculous cycle of crazy workload I've allowed myself to get into. I have to ask for help.

Find Your Safe People

I identify someone I respect and trust – in this case, the deputy head. There are people like this in every school – find yours. 'The highs, the lows, the struggles – there's nobody to share it with!' I blurt through snot and tears. If you haven't snotted in an office somewhere at the beginning of your career, you've barely lived.

'Share it with the students!' he says. This has stayed with me since. This advice comes with an important note of caution: I am not advocating you share your relationship dramas, your latest house move or your gynaecological issues with your Year 9 class. I am suggesting that you let them know you're human – if you're disappointed, you can say so. When you're proud, you can let it show. If someone has stolen all of the wheels from your car that morning, which is the reason you're late for school (true story), there's no reason they can't share in your indignation (and tell you that your choice of car was rubbish in the first place).

It's My Birthday!

January 2000. It's my birthday. Nobody at school knows this. I lumber through the day in a mire of self-pity. It's period five. There are two Year 10 girls in the front of my classroom, whose every detail I remember to this day, let us call them Harmony and Tori. Harmony and Tori, who scare the bejesus out of me with their feisty manner, big earrings, lacquered hair and utter loathing for German, are carrying on their conversation as if I'm not there. N.B. Being ignored is generally worse than being sworn at.

The dam finally bursts. 'BUT IT'S MY BIRTHDAY!' I shout.

Brief, startled pause. Then, 'Why didn't you tell us?' Perfect excuse to graffiti 'Alles Gute zum Geburtstag' (Happy Birthday) all over the board, but hey, they learned four words of German that day and their greeting is warm. I have made it my policy ever since to tell everybody I meet at school when it's my birthday – and bring cake, as they do in Germany. German cake, for cultural learning options.

Find an Incentive

Bottom set Year 11 are a formative experience for me in my NQT year. I am very proud of myself – I've put into place a lesson structure which involved getting the core learning done then having a 'choice' of activities, including the 'magazine corner', which has actual bean bags.

I've been to Germany and picked up a load of German teenage magazines. To my astonishment, it works! Students romp through their verb tables and sports vocabulary, demand their sticker (no child is ever too old for stickers) and take themselves quietly into the 'magazine corner' to imbibe German culture and absorb new language.

Germans, you will know if you've been there, are rather less prudish than we Brits. So perhaps I shouldn't really be that surprised when, clearing my classroom after a smug term of successfully teaching this group, I pick up the pile of magazines to find that each and every one has a centre-fold of a full-frontal naked picture in the middle.

Still, one declared, 'Ich habe meine schwester gegessen' (I ate my sister for breakfast) in his German speaking exam, so something stuck...

It takes more than a year. I'd love to say that I was a fully formed, competent teacher by the end of that year of fumbling and mistakes, but, as the title of this book indicates, it doesn't work like this.

I remember a colleague using the 'three years' mantra which I continue to repeat unashamedly. For most new teachers, the second year is a little more straightforward – things aren't quite as exhaustingly new; in the third year, your confidence really grows. For this reason, I continue to urge caution with even the most talented and ambitious when it comes to taking on responsibility too soon. If you can really enjoy that confidence of the third year, then do.

In fact, I scuppered that for myself by completely changing contexts in 2001. I fell in love and moved to London.

It's 2001. I move from being a rural, language colleague in the countryside to an inner-city comprehensive in Camden – at the time, widely (and with a note of pride) known to be the 'lowest achieving school in Camden'. The building has the appearance of a Victorian workhouse and there's barbed wire on the top of every external wall. My mum drives up to see where I was working and admits to crying later, when she sees where her daughter has ended up.

Guess what, reader? I was pig in sh*t happy for my five years there. The context that's right for you changes with time and is not always the one you'd expect. The school had the highest number of refugees of any school in Europe and, quite literally, provided a 'refuge' for almost 100 different nationalities. There was a work-hard, play-hard culture and parties that left the headteacher not speaking to any of us for days at a time (neighbours, noise, bulldozers... don't ask) – he always forgave us, of course.

Was it easy? Erm...

Finding Your Teacher Identity Takes Time

Month two in my new school. My head of department is a formidable woman whom I respect to this day. Children do not breathe without her permission. 'Did I ask you to speak?' is a phrase from her that I use to this day. I observe her teaching a lesson on hobbies in German. It is seamless – just brilliant. I make dedicated, copious notes and leave the room to enter my own classroom and replicate her skill.

Within five minutes, Hailey has picked up a table and hurled it across the room at Andy, calling him a c**t after he disrespected her mother (the worst fight I ever witnessed was the result of one child saying to another: 'Your mum's got three legs'). Within 20 minutes, the cavalry had been called to restore order and I am, again, hiccoughing in the office with full snot and tears.

I was not my head of department – her methods in the classroom were not mine. Observe others, listen to others, then cherry-pick what works for you. Don't be afraid to reject what doesn't. And don't worry, fights in most schools these days are relatively rare.

Was it all fights and snot? Of course it wasn't. Once I did find my identity in the classroom (a mix of humour and kindness with disappointment a far more powerful tool than anger – and shouting just makes me stressed), being in the classroom became the very definition of being 'in my element' – to this day, in mid-flow in a lesson, I forget time, forget everything. We laugh, we make mistakes, we learn. I remain mentor to many of these students, now in their 30s, to this day. They taught me more about the world, its tragedies and joys, its conflicts and kindnesses, than any adult ever could, and the richness of my career is thanks to them. On the day of the London bombings, we unquestioningly stayed in school late into the night to ensure each and every child and their families were safe.

We went to Germany in the end. We also went to France, Italy and Spain together. Children who had never left London splashed gleefully in the sea on the Costa Brava and sailed in banana boats off the coast of the South of France. If you get the chance to take children on a trip abroad, despite all the red tape, do it! What other job gives you joy like that?

Dr Emma Kell
Education Consultant, trainer of teachers, writer and speaker

SARAH MULLIN

Ten Tips for Early Career Teachers

Congratulations on becoming a teacher. You have chosen one of the most important jobs there is – the profession that creates all other professions. You will be shaping the hearts and minds of children for the rest of their lives. You will be helping them to maximise their learning potential. You will be giving children and young people the very best start in life, helping them to realise their aspirations. It's important to enjoy your journey, embrace the opportunities that are available, appreciate the positive moments and reward yourself for a job well done.

Here are ten little tips to help you as you enter a career with limitless opportunities.

1. Celebrate the Little Wins

Working in education means working towards goals such as statutory examinations and end of unit assessments. Sometimes we become so focused on those end results that we forget to celebrate the little wins that happen every single day in our schools. Don't forget to celebrate the first time a student achieves something that they couldn't do before. It's a cause for celebration when a child who has been struggling to form friendships starts socialising with their peers. Don't forget to celebrate your own little wins too. Did your lively class of students respond well to a new behaviour strategy you tried? Tweet your success stories – it's encouraging and uplifting to see early career teachers doing well. There's always a reason to celebrate, try and find the positive every single day.

2. Establish Positive Relationships

Establishing positive relationships with your students, parents and colleagues will be central to your success as a teacher. Get to know each and every child; work closely with parents and carers so that everyone can share in the child's learning journey. By getting to know the needs, motivations and aspirations of the children you teach, you can maximise the learning potential of every single child.

Positive relationships allow us to collaborate and work together more effectively. Schools thrive because there's a strong team of staff working together. Where would we be without our caretakers, admin staff, teaching assistants and cooks; our lunch time supervisors, cleaners, finance team and librarians? It's always nice to show appreciation for those you work with; we could not do our jobs without their support.

3. Ask for Help

Never be afraid to ask for help, advice or clarification. By striving to learn, grow and develop as a professional, you are showing that you are committed to becoming the best teacher you can be. Our children and young people deserve to have teachers just like you who are endeavouring to provide the best possible learning experiences. Remember that every single person who has contributed to this book was, at the beginning of their career, where you are now. We understand and recognise your excitement, your nerves and your ambitions. We appreciate that you will have worries too, so please reach out and ask for help.

4. Be Flexible

No two days in the world of education are ever the same! It is so important to be flexible and adaptable. You might have planned the most brilliant lesson and have a carefully crafted to-do list for the day ahead, and then a child comes to school in tears because they have a relative who's unwell, or another child has forgotten their PE kit. Suddenly, it's the end of the day and you haven't managed half of what you'd planned. It happens to all of us and I can assure you that things do get easier. As a teacher, you'll become a master at prioritising and multi-tasking; you'll have mentors and colleagues who'll lift you up when times are tough. Although we are always striving for excellence, remember that sometimes good just has to be good enough.

5. Stay Positive

If you've had a challenging lesson, and we have all been there, please try to stay positive. If you're feeling disappointed or deflated, please know that you're in the right job because you truly care. Reflect on your experiences, consider strategies you've tried that you will use again, and think about alternative approaches that you might wish to adopt moving forward. Take advantage of the brilliant support systems and resources that are available for early career teachers and listen to podcasts. If you can, try to attend some conferences and educational events where you can engage with other teaching professionals. The very best teachers are always growing, always developing and always learning.

6. Take Care of Yourself

One of my favourite quotes is 'you can't pour from an empty cup, take care of yourself first'. This is probably the best advice I can give to you as teachers, but I can tell you first-hand that it can be incredibly hard to do! As teachers, we never stop caring, but we must take the time to look after ourselves, so that we are best placed to support our students who need us.

7. Invest in Your Health

Never underestimate the power of a good night's sleep. When it's late in the evening and you've got a pile of exercise books to mark and an inbox full of emails to respond to, think about what your little learners need most. A teacher who's enthusiastic and full of passion, ready to impart their knowledge because they're well rested... or the alternative? Your wellbeing matters because you matter. Invest in yourself and your health.

8. Collaboration NOT Competition

If you've ever been to a conference where I've been presenting or if you follow me on social media, you'll hear me say these three little words a lot: collaboration NOT competition. We are all in this together. When teachers unite, amazing things happen. There are so many teachers sharing their brilliant resources online – adapt them so that they are suitable for your learners in your setting. There's no better resource in education than the skills and experiences of each other: share good practice, observe one another, build your professional networks both online and in real life. Surround yourself with people who bring out the best in you, find those positive, uplifting people who believe in you, who support you and will even challenge you to become the best version of yourself.

9. Celebrate Being a Teacher

We can all help to show the world how fantastic it is to be a teacher. Do 'talk up' our profession to others in conversations and on social media; celebrate your achievements. Share the joy of being a teacher.

10. Enjoy the Journey

I'd like to wish you the very best of luck in your future careers in education. Enjoy every single moment. Your children and young people will remember you for the rest of their lives. Being a teacher comes with a lot of responsibility but reaps so many rewards.

Welcome to our wonderful profession.

Sarah Mullin
Deputy Headteacher, The Priory, Edgbaston

DAME ALISON PEACOCK

Reminiscences

My summer term teaching practice took place in a small primary school in Coventry. I do not recall ever watching Mr Scoop, the dour class teacher, working with his class, although I guess I must have experienced this. His was a Year 4 class and suddenly they were handed over to me for the summer term and I became their teacher. Unless there was an inordinate amount of noise, no one came near. There were no plans, no schemes of work, curriculum maps had not been invented. However, over the Easter holidays, I carefully prepared a topic web which required me to link all of the subjects where possible to a central theme. I decided to plan lessons all linked to the overall topic of 'Water'.

At the time, I was living with a group of students and as I became more and more immersed in my work in school, our flat began to be filled with the paraphernalia of primary teaching. I would entertain my flatmates, all of whom were supposed to be engaged in deeply serious postgraduate study, with stories of what had happened during the day in school. We all got involved in the student kitchen (three men and me) building sand and water clocks, which subsequently the children created in lessons where there was a spurious connection between junk modelling, teaching the mathematical concept of time and my chosen 'Water' topic for the term.

I was keen to provide first-hand experiences for these inner-city children and thought the more that I could bring learning to life and avoid worksheets, the better my teaching would be. I soon found that some areas of the curriculum are easier to teach and to resource than others.

In maths, every child had a textbook and workbook I recall, so when they weren't building timers and 'clocks' they probably practised some maths.

In English, I read them a story about the impact of a huge flood on a village, we wrote about this, talked a lot and read lots more stories and poems. PE was mainly taken up with getting changed, walking to the school hall and dodging the squashed peas on the floor, left over from lunch when the hall was used as a dining room. Sometimes, if we could book the hall, we would engage in drama and imagine ourselves in a huge range of situations, often stimulated by our stories. When the weather was good, we went outside and played rounders. In art, we got the paints out and made rich, colourful pictures which I carefully displayed around the room.

Science was the area of the curriculum where I was completely unsure what to teach but knew I wanted it to involve active learning. I hoped the children would get excited about using magnifying glasses – I knew this subject should be all about enquiry, close observation and discovery. What to teach? There were no books, no records of any previous science lessons and we needed to link everything back to the central topic of 'Water'. Aha! Looking around the student kitchen, I decided that for my first discovery lesson I would bring in a range of materials so that the children could hypothesise what would happen to each material when water was added. The idea was that each group would record the material, predict what would happen and then note what actually occurred. I brought in salt, sugar, tea bags, flour and brown sauce. All of which would probably have been fine. In my enthusiasm, however, I wanted to give them as great a range as possible so, looking further in the kitchen cupboards, I decided to also add washing powder, washing-up liquid, baking powder and rice. As I proudly set up this lesson during playtime, I remember thinking that this class would remember me for my imaginative lessons. I was now truly a teacher.

Everything started well. The children listened carefully and regarded the containers they had on each group table with interest. I told them that scientists make careful observations and learn from what they see. The groups set to work, and I wandered around encouraging and generally feeling pleased with the hive of activity. Things began to go wrong when Andrew decided that his group should introduce a taste test. Not only would they watch what happened when they added salt to water, for example, they would taste it. Others noticed this strategy. Too late, I implored the children not to drink any of the concoctions they were making. In those days, children went home for lunch. On this particular day several did not return, complaining of stomach aches 'because Miss poisoned us'. I was reprimanded by the Year 4 teacher who – having been disturbed in the staffroom by several calls from angry parents – asked me not to feed anything to the children during the rest of my teaching practice. He then returned to his chair. Chastened, I decided that in future, instead of planning pseudo-chemistry science lessons, I would call upon my biology experience and plan an enquiry related to wildlife and nature.

A few weeks went by and then I discovered that there was a small pond in a park nearby the school. How brilliant would it be if the children, with nets and buckets, could take part in pond dipping? This would link perfectly to our topic for the term and we would be able to identify the wildlife. Perfect. I set about persuading Mr Scoop. At that time, in the same way that there were no curriculum plans, there were no risk-assessments either. Off we went to the park one morning, excitedly carrying pond dipping gear. The school did not have any nets, but a couple of the children had some, and I managed to buy a few from a camping shop in the city. We probably had one net between three children, along with buckets and containers. Mr Scoop came with us.

When we arrived at the pond, I quickly realised that 30 children around the edge of open water, all vying to catch whatever they could and transfer it to an open bucket, was probably slightly more problematic than I had anticipated. However, all went well and we began to find all kinds of pondlife including beetles, sticklebacks and all manner of other interesting tiny creatures. We stopped for a while to have some biscuits and orange squash in the sunshine and then returned to school triumphantly carrying our buckets, now heavier with water, so that we could explore further in the classroom with our magnifying glasses and sketch books. We left the buckets on the desks and went off for lunch. Later, I planned to drive back to the park and return the contents of each bucket to the pond.

As I approached the classroom after lunch, I heard a squeal. Several of the children, so excited by the morning's events, had crept back into the classroom to see how the contents of their buckets were enjoying their new surroundings. What I had not realised was that when the nets scraped along the bottom of the pond some of what was collected was mud. Within the mud, it transpired, there were small, black, slimy leeches. During the hour of lunch, some of these leeches in the buckets had edged their way up the sides of each container. Indeed, not only had they leeched up the sides of the buckets, a fair few had landed not only on, but also in, the desks and were now to be found amongst the children's books.

Luckily, Andrew was not afraid of leeches. I was grateful when he offered to search through desks and replace the escapees back in the buckets. The rest of the afternoon went well and it was only at the end of the day, as I loaded the buckets into the boot of my car, that I realised I was going to need to drive very, very slowly.

All too quickly, it seemed, my teaching practice ended. I had enjoyed getting to know each child and there was definitely a much livelier energy in the room than when I had arrived. Mr Scoop signed off my teaching practice and recommended that I should pass my PGCE. As I left on the final day, he offered a few words of advice. Mainly, it would appear, he felt I would be a good teacher as long as I remembered to keep my classroom tidy. At which point, he illustrated his comment by pointing to a pile of maths textbooks that somehow had been relegated to the floor in a corner so that the shelf could be taken up with a wide range of strangely constructed sand timers. I apologised to Mr Scoop, gathered up my belongings and my flowers from the children and began the drive home. Little did I realise that a particularly persistent leech was making its way up the back of my driving seat, heading with determination towards the skin on my neck...

The remainder of my teaching career has continued in the same vein. Many joyful times, full of hard work, risk-taking and laughter; with the occasional 'leech on the back of your neck' moment. Good luck as you join our wonderful profession and pursue the best job in the world.

Dame Alison Peacock
Chief Executive of the Chartered College of Teaching

HALIL TAMGUMUS

A Culture of Belonging

Education.

This is the answer to the following question – How can we create a more tolerant and open-minded society?

Teachers.

This is the answer to the next question – Who is best placed to make the changes needed?

When I first started teaching all those years ago back in 2005, all I wanted to do was teach. It sounds a bit silly when I read that back. Why did I get in to teaching if I did not want to teach? What I mean is, it did not matter what I taught – I just wanted to get the information from the curriculum to the children. I wanted to make sure that they moved up to Year 5 with all the knowledge that was expected of them from Year 4.

By the way, I will digress a little here, but it is relevant: my first class was a Year 4 class in a school only a stone's throw away from the school where I am currently the headteacher. That was almost 15 years ago, and I still remember the children in that class. There is a special bond with your very first class that cannot be replicated. I had so much fun teaching them.

I had a puppet that I would use to 'help' explain things to the children. Looking back, it was probably the creepiest puppet I could have chosen. He (it was a boy) had a wide, toothless grin and eyes that were far, far too intense. To top it off, he had the worst Sheffield accent ever. I studied in

Sheffield for four years – I consider it my second home. Beautiful scenery, beautiful people, and a beautiful accent – well it is beautiful when I am not trying to imitate it.

The enjoyment I was gaining from basically being a fool and laughing at myself meant that the children could do the same. It was a safe space for them. Their personalities developed; they were not afraid to get things wrong. They were incredible. I still think about them fondly. My favourite ever end of year gift was given to me from that class. A mug from a young man called Michael. It was actually a glass tankard with the words 'The Best Man' inscribed on it in gold (it was clearly for a best man at a wedding). Without him knowing what the gift was actually for, he looked up at me and said:

'You are the best man to me!' – that will stay with me forever.

I made the children feel as though they were part of something. This runs through my whole philosophy as an educationalist. Belonging. It is one of four words that make up my current school's core values. Belong, Care, Persevere and Succeed.

Why is this so important to me? Belonging, to feel part of something?

The answer is simple – I did not have that sense of belonging at school. Mainly at secondary school but also at primary school. My sister and I were the only Turkish children (Turkish Cypriot to be precise) that attended our secondary school, we were also part of the very low percentage of BAME children. I distinctly remember feeling othered. I clearly remember feeling different. I cannot remember learning anything that was remotely linked to who I was (who I am) – a person from a different culture.

I was a well-behaved boy at school, a little cheeky, quite charming (it states this in my school report in Year 8) and a bit of a joker. I was by no means the cleverest child in the school, but I had some intelligence (some may say otherwise – do not listen to them! Lies, all lies).

But I still managed to fail almost all of my GCSEs. If I remember correctly, I got a B in English literature – a subject I enjoyed. I enjoyed it because I got to read about other places, other backgrounds. Stories that would fire my imagination!

I was taught by teachers who did not allow me to be me. I had a dual identity (a bit like Superman... ok, not like Superman at all). At home, I was a Turkish Cypriot boy enveloped in a rich culture, surrounded by family, food and tradition. Whilst at school, I was not. I did not talk about my heritage or my background. This was in part due to the lack of interest from teachers and the lack of representation in the curriculum but mainly due to the racist abuse I knew I would endure.

I often wonder what school would have been like if I could have safely and confidently shared who I was. If the curriculum reflected me in some way, I would have felt valued and other children would have learned something new.

I wish my education growing up made me feel like I belonged, that I was part of something bigger as a seen individual.

Giving children the safe space to feel that they can share who they are, to share their stories and their culture is so important. You have to model this – give yourself to them. Share with them.

Shape the curriculum to mirror the children that you teach and reflect the society to which they will contribute in the future. By creating an inclusive curriculum, you not only make those children who are from different cultures feel they belong but you expose those children who are white British to different cultures and backgrounds, thus creating the conditions for tolerance and open mindedness to bloom and flourish.

This could be as simple as making sure that for every time you discuss or teach the children about a famous scientist or author that you counter that stereotype with another scientist or author from a different culture, with a different skin colour or a different gender. When teaching the works of Shakespeare, why not share the compositions of Rumi?

It is important to state that I do not advocate removing the figures being taught about currently in our schools. I promote the need to teach our children a truer picture of the past. A past that is not just retold through one lens but is viewed through multiple lenses. A truth that is balanced and just.

This is not idealistic; this is not beyond our reach. With every year you teach, you have the chance to create a future generation that accepts and celebrates difference.

See their culture, see their colour, see the child.

Halil Tamgumus
Headteacher, Braunstone Community Primary School, Leicester

PROFESSOR SAM TWISELTON OBE

Words of Wisdom

When I give advice to anyone who works in school (whatever their role, level, stage of career or the phase/subject they work with), I like to start in the same place. This is to remind them why they chose the career in the first place. I ask them why their job gets them up in the morning. I nearly always find we basically share the same thoughts; on a good day – a day when it's not just about paying the mortgage or catching up on gossip – I'm talking about the days when we know we're doing something important, that matters, that makes a difference.

The words and phrases about why I love my job that pop into my mind include just that – it is about making a difference, but also the why and the how? It is because we all know that ultimately education in all its forms has the power to transform lives, open gateways, change individuals, the communities they live in, society, the world! Without education we would not have any of the other things our civilised lives depend on.

Goodness, how recent times have shown us the importance of this. Obviously, we cannot take it for granted that this is what we will achieve, and we need to be very alert to the risks of getting it wrong and making it worse. Just as most of us can remember teachers who touched our lives in a good way, we can usually think of those where it was the opposite. But basically, most people who work in education, and that's probably everyone reading this, are in it for the same reasons and that is what unites us, inspires us, gets us out of bed.

As you face the daily challenges of being a new teacher, it is so easy to lose sight of these important things – to not be able to see the wood for the trees. It is worth trying to develop a habit of regularly reminding yourself of these realities – sometimes it will help you prioritise and decide how best to use your time and effort.

As always, with anything important, education is going to be one of the most crucial features of the rebuilding (and maybe even to some extent reimagining) of our communities and society going forward.

In a new, post-Covid-19 world it is very likely that all in school – from new teachers to senior leaders – will be inevitably and rightly focused on very practical issues. Establishing new routines, relationships and ways of working with pupils who have had a long period away from school will be top priority. For some children, these will include circumstances involving a range of trauma. Addressing these challenges will be 'all hands on deck' in this endeavour. If this is done in a culture of teamwork and mutual support, my prediction is that this will make a conducive and supportive context for new entrants to the profession. To get through this initial period in a culture of support and pragmatism seems sensible. As a new teacher, throwing yourself into the spirit of working together and being flexible and responsive as circumstances change should quickly help you to feel as though you belong. This is one of the most important factors in helping you to enjoy your job.

It is important also to be proactive about seeking support. Put time into understanding the different areas of expertise and types of personalities of those around you. You will find you need different types of support at different times. It is so helpful if you have developed a wide range of relationships that you can draw on for different things – whether it is advice about pupil behaviour or a shoulder to cry on.

From my own personal experience, I suggest you work out where the positive and negative energy resides in the staffroom. While everyone can have a bad day and therefore need to offload, there are some who make too much of a habit of it.

In the autumn term of my NQT year, I found myself part of a small group who found fault with absolutely everything and it was very easy just to join in. I realised after a few weeks that it was making me dread going into the staffroom and I made a conscious effort to avoid those conversations in the future and to spend more time with cheerier colleagues. It made such a difference, and from that point onwards I have always tried to avoid getting sucked into negative spirals with 'dementors'.

As things settle to a new normal, the foundation of relationships and teamwork that has been established during this strange period we are living through will hopefully really benefit you for years to come.

Professor Sam Twiselton OBE
Director of Education, Sheffield Hallam University

CHAPTER 1

My First Four and a Half Years

Setting the Scene of My First Five Years

Times have changed so much over the years. When I started teaching in 1965, there was no help at all. I clearly remember being abandoned in an art room with a register and left to get on with it. No one offered advice and I knew no one to ask. It was a 700-pupil secondary school with a head, two deputies and 50 members of staff. I cannot remember any of them asking if I was alright or if I needed help. I had never marked a register before, my blackboard writing wobbled and I had planned no lessons as I had not been given a timetable.

I do remember being petrified. Nothing I had done at school or at college seemed to have prepared me adequately for this. I stood and looked at a class, sometimes in abject fear, not knowing what to say or do. Some 'lessons' proved totally unsuitable for the age of the groups they were prepared for and some were completed in 15 minutes with nothing else prepared to last the rest of the hour. I didn't *feel* like a teacher, I didn't *think* like a teacher and I didn't *look* like a teacher.

Worst of all, I didn't know how a 21-year-old teacher was supposed to feel, think or look and the school seemed to be populated with 'old' teachers so I had no immediate role models.

It didn't help that I didn't have any 'real' clothes suitable for a teacher, I keenly felt that my image was all wrong – I had never planned on teaching. Female teachers were not allowed to wear any form of trousers in school at that time, with the exception of PE teachers who were allowed to wear track suit bottoms in winter. As students, we were cut some slack, but now it was 'for real'. Every day was a dilemma of what to wear, with the only two skirts I possessed both being very short and tight. Today, everyone is used to seeing women of all ages in fairly short, tight skirts, but in the 1960s it was only the younger generations and so – even on such a large staff – it was me, alone. My summer tops were basically different forms of T-shirts, mainly baggy and worn – and in winter I wore the same big home-knitted jumpers I had sported in college. Money was short and cheaper clothing was confined to the big cities. There was no internet, of course, and on a salary of £45 a month after tax, it was a long time before I could afford to make myself more presentable.

How I wish I had asked family for contributions to my wardrobe for my birthday when I knew I had been appointed. How *you* feel about your appearance is important (although you should not worry about what others think) and getting it right can be a big help. I was demoralised enough in those first months in the profession and worrying about my perceived unprofessional image only compounded the low self-esteem.

My register class was a Year 8 class of 12 to 13 year olds and the day was full of ringing bells. One bell brought the pupils in at 9am and one signalled us to go to the hall for assembly – a daily event led by the head wearing his graduation gown. The students stood in rows and sang two hymns accompanied by a woman on the grand piano. Then the head read a passage from the Bible, everyone said the Lord's Prayer and we filed back out again. It was about as spiritual as a visit to the doctors. As this was going on, the second deputy head, Basher Burgess, was roaming up and down the rows of students, punching them in the kidneys and growling: 'Jesus loves yer,' in their ears. Periodically, he would fling an arm towards the double doors and a troublesome child would shuffle out to join the ever increasing line-up outside his office and and – when assembly was over – Basher would fetch his cane and give each pupil three strokes on each hand. It was clearly a highly effective form of behaviour management as it was almost always the same pupils there the next day and the day after...

The final bell at the start of the day told register classes to go to their first lesson and I waited to see who would arrive in my room for their double period art lesson. In the end, I sent a student to the office to ask if I could please have a timetable so that I could be better prepared.

There were three art rooms, two were adjacent with a shared stock room between them and one – that of the head of art – was at the other end of the school. He never came down to my art room in the four and a half years I was there, and we never had a team meeting. Gordon was in the adjacent room to mine and I didn't even meet him until my second week. I was petrified. I hid in my room and quaked. Classes came and went. Most of them were quite co-operative but I did have run-ins with the Year 10s on many occasions. They were leaving at the end of the year and were demob happy from my very first day in September. I didn't know what to do about them and had no one to ask. I began to dread their lessons, the rudeness, occasional missiles flung and the loud conversations across the room. When I plucked up the courage to ask Gordon about it after a month he just laughed and said Year 10s were always like that every year, but I couldn't hear any noise coming from his end of the stockroom. There were no policies for guidance and no detentions.

The staffroom was large and full of easy chairs, usually in two circles with a single line round the extremities. I was totally ignored for the first two months and dreaded going in there. People appeared to have their own seats and sat in the same place at both break and lunch time. My first visit resulted in a rather large lady saying, 'That's Dennis's seat!' quite sharply when I went to sit down. Lunch was served in the hall and was equally traumatic. I hadn't the courage to walk straight to the front of the long queue and could waste most of my lunch time waiting to be served. I soon abandoned school lunches and took a sandwich, which I ate in my art room, alone.

Building strong relationships with your colleagues is important. We all need to feel a part of something, we need friendship and a smile from time to time. We also need to have colleagues we can trust and whose advice we can seek. Professor Sam Twiselton has written about 'getting in with the wrong crowd' in her contribution, to be found in the opening section of the book. In a large school that is an easy mistake to make – there are always a few grumblers and dissenters in a staffroom. Unfortunately, in the last full-time post I held in a primary school in Kirklees, the dissenters were led by the deputy head! I didn't 'get in' with anyone, grumblers or otherwise.

Leadership of a school is so important for newly qualified teachers. There was no leadership in my first experience of teaching – it was every one for themselves. I struggled, but I certainly wasn't the worst. I remember passing poor Mr Baum's class with horror. He had first years – aged 11 to 12 – and first years were with one teacher for all lessons except PE and science. Mr Baum's class was totally out of control, missiles flew round the room and children climbed on chairs and desks while he stood – red faced and apoplectic – at the front trying to shout above the noise. He was a mature man who had trained late and this was his second year at the school. He left the profession at the end of my first year.

What I soon learned in that first school was that you can't win by trying to out-shout pupils from challenging backgrounds. That first school was located in a small coal mining town, in the days when the pits were still open. In those days, the narrow streets were lined almost exclusively with two-bedroom, red brick terrace houses within which there were often two or three adults and three or four or more children. Life was crowded and noisy and frequently tempers would flare. Our students knew all about how to win by shouting… they knew less about how to respond to calm and peace and praise and kindness, so focusing on those qualities, and praising pupils who responded, was far more effective. Yet I still struggled, and there were many days when I stood in despair at the front of a noisy rabble and didn't know whether to scream or cry.

Gradually, however, I made a few friends, earned my own seat in the staffroom and started to feel more a part of things. Perhaps I had been giving off the wrong vibes and that deterred staff from speaking? But I never found a mentor to advise me and support me in my early, blindfolded venture into the profession.

How I Bumbled My Way into Teaching

How could I go through three years at teacher training college and come out at the other end ignorant and totally unprepared for the job? There are three answers to that question.

The first thing to say is that I never wanted to be a teacher. I disliked teachers and schools intensely due to my own personal experience as a pupil in both primary and secondary school. My family circumstances deteriorated due to the death of my father when I was five, after he had spent two years in bed totally paralysed following a stroke. Mother was left with four children aged five to ten and no income in the days before widow's pension or any sort of state benefit. In order to keep us all together, we moved to a huge Victorian semi-detached and took in six students from Leeds University. Life was hard and during the lengthy holidays we were quite impoverished. Sadly, I became quite dirty and neglected. The primary school I attended was quite 'middle class' and gradually I became isolated and lonely, and acquired the label 'stink bomb'.

Secondary school was a little better as I learned to keep myself clean and tidy, and my two older sisters were already in the school. However, I was already disaffected and – although I was able enough to keep my place in the 'A' class of four streams – I didn't work hard and I didn't get on with many of the staff. It is a sad indictment of the profession to admit that, when on a day's professional development, we were asked to think of the most inspirational teacher we had ever met during our own time at school, I was the only one of the 60 on the Kirklees Local Authority team unable to find one inspirational teacher from my personal past.

My one passion at the girls' high school was art. In those days, I thought I was quite good at art and it led to me really wanting to leave high school at the end of Year 11 to go to Leeds Art College in order to become a commercial artist. However, when I informed the school of this midway through Year 11, I was summoned to the headteacher's office and she reduced me to tears with a mix of sarcasm and ridicule. It transpired that no one left an 'A' class without completing sixth form and going to university. If I persisted in my application, she would tell the college the 'truth' about me as a scholar, but if I stayed on for sixth form, she would give me a reasonable reference. It was all about the numbers in a sixth form for funding in those days.

I stayed on.

Part way through the first year of sixth form, however, I discovered that I could enter teacher training college with just six O-levels and no A-levels (I had scraped eight GCEs) at the end of first year sixth form due to the difference in age specification for entry. To start school, the age requirement was to be aged five by the start of the September of that school year. To enter college, the age requirement was to be 18 by the end of September. My birthday is in September – I had always been the oldest at school and now I was to be the youngest at college.

So, I escaped school early after all and ended up training for a profession I had no intention of pursuing in the future.

The final factor was that, due to the massive snows of 1963 and my partner-in-crime, who was on first teaching practice in the same rural primary school as myself, we managed to get through the second term's teaching placement by not arriving at the school until 10.30 in the morning and leaving again at 2.30 in the afternoon, thus only teaching one real lesson a day. Ron, the minibus driver, was amazingly receptive to bribery and so we achieved being last to be dropped off in the morning (after enjoying a mug of steaming hot tea in a transport café with Ron) and the first to be picked up in the afternoon, even though we were not 'at the end of the line'. We arrived at school with tales of being stuck in snow drifts or blocked by others stuck in the snow. A packet of cigarettes a week for our driver certainly did the business!

Our second teaching practice was in the final year, and this time I was on my own in a secondary school. This could have been regarded as a realistic introduction to 'the other side of the desk' as the experience was very similar to my first true post two terms later. The head of art spent my lessons in the staffroom and was quite disparaging about my outcomes yet offered no help at all – and I asked for none. I made no friends, and nobody gave me any advice. My teaching was mediocre, and I learned little from the experience – and especially because halfway through I was taken ill in school and sent home (a journey of which I have no memory). The next day mother called for the doctor and he came twice in four hours as he was so worried. My right arm and side were temporarily paralysed. Sufficient to say I missed over three weeks of the practice, and was threatened with a repeat of my third year as no one could miss longer than one week, but thanks to the senior lecturer at college, I was given a reprieve.

The amazing thing is that I entered a profession I disliked intensely, without any desire to teach at all, and with scarcely any actual teaching experience under my belt, but as soon as I discovered that you could treat pupils and learning in quite the opposite way to the way I was taught, I grew to love it and have loved it ever since.

I learned to model my practice on the teachers I admired most, I learned confidence and approachability, and most of all, I learned to ask for help when I needed it, even if it was never offered. Watching and learning from others is a great way to get started – you will soon adapt and customise your practice to reflect your personal preferences and style.

Departing from My First Post

A final complication in my early career was my chosen means of transport to school – a Honda 50 – a very small motor scooter, quite new to the scene at the time.

When I accepted the job at the secondary school, I hadn't thought about how I would get there. It was a shock, therefore, to discover that the journey would involve a 20-minute bus ride to Wakefield bus station and then a change of buses for a 35-minute ride to Normanton followed by a ten-minute walk to the school. With delays and waits for buses, a total of up to one and a half hours at the beginning and end of each day. I only tried it once before school opened to know it was not feasible for a reluctant traveller, so I went to a garage in Wakefield and came out with a brand-new scooter bought on credit.

I loved that machine! I practised conscientiously prior to the first day of term and found I could complete the whole journey in anywhere between 30 and 45 minutes. Perfect! It would have helped if I had known what time teachers usually started at schools in those days (not nearly as early as they do today), so I made a guesstimate and roared into the front gates at 20 to 9 of day one! That was *not* early enough – even for the '60s – as a really angry faced woman standing with folded arms and legs akimbo on the top step of the main entrance informed me in no uncertain terms.

Very Angry Lady did not introduce herself by either name or post, she did not shake my hand or welcome me to the school or the profession. She snarled:

'Follow me!' and I grabbed my bags and followed her, helmet flaps flapping, down two corridors, through a hall, down a third corridor and round a corner where she opened the door on the left, virtually pushed me in, thrust a register at me, and growled:

'This is your room, this is your register,' and left.

That lady never spoke to me again in the four and a half years I was at the school. She was the first deputy head. Actually – that was not true – she did turn back at the door and snap:

'And shift that wretched machine from the front of the school and never park it there again!'

Riding a small scooter not built to travel at more than 50 miles an hour may be a pleasure on most summer and early autumn days, but in the depths of winter it is often a horror. I would arrive at school battered and bedraggled, often soaking wet and very cold. I couldn't afford (and probably wouldn't have worn) suitable waterproofs for the job, and a duffle coat and helmet are not the most protective all-weather wear.

I often set off a little late and would be pushing the small machine beyond its capacity, hurtling round bends as though I was in the TT on the Isle of Man. I had many near misses but only actually fell off once, skidding sideways in heavy rain on the top of the moorland – much to the pleasure, it seemed, of the gentleman following me in a small, grey car. He parked close to me, got out and greeted me (still lying on the road in the rain) with the words:

'I knew you were going to fall off, you were riding much too fast.'

Luckily, I was completely alright except for one grazed leg, but it did take some of the fun out of my future journeys. I also got tired of the endless jokes on the playground and in the staffroom about Batman, Super Woman, Ros Sheene or Ros Dunlop (after two famous motorcyclists), Chug Chug Girl, Ros the Drip and so on and so on…

After four and a half years, I had had enough of the travel and was seeking a job nearer to home.

My Top Tips for Starting a New Post

- Remember that everyone struggles in some areas at the beginning, persevere – it will all come right in the end.
- Keep calm or at least fake calmness!
- Praise those children who work hard and behave, and ignore those who don't – unless there is danger!
- Ask for help if no one has offered it.
- Accept all the help you can get and listen to your mentor and others.
- Make friends and ask them for advice when you need it.
- Buy a couple of appropriate professional outfits and a change of shirts/tops to accompany them – dress to feel good about yourself.
- Consider your journey to school before accepting a post. Many new teachers need to accept the first job they are offered, but you still need to take care of yourself and – if you can afford it – a small car is still the best means if public transport is too challenging. After a few weeks, you will probably be able to agree a car share with another member of staff for the environment's sake.

CHAPTER 2

First Primary Experience

Starting as a new and still-learning girl at a single form entry primary school was as different, but as strange, an experience as my first four and a half years had been. Every change of stage and type of school, as opposed to internal moves in the same school, will come with its own difficulties, no matter how much you look forward to and embrace the change.

Small schools have an intimacy amongst the staff that can be a huge strength and driving force for the school, but when they go wrong...

Maybe my reasons for moving were little better than my reasons for my first post had been, but there are often personal motivations in moves between schools, and that can be a huge positive because you are usually achieving what you wanted to achieve. I had wanted to move to primary because I found I did not enjoy the comings and goings of classes every day of the week, and my beloved art had become boring after three years with no fresh ideas or stimulation. There was absolutely no in-service professional development for anyone at all in those days – once you qualified that was it. There was also no internet of course, so other than buying books – which I couldn't afford – it was enforced stagnation. However I did grow very fond of my register classes, seen twice a day, and would have loved to teach them myself. I also wanted to be nearer to home and avoid that formidable journey through another winter.

The fact that a post became available in the village where we lived was just – to me at the time – a miraculous coincidence. I knew nothing about the school, had no networks in the village and made no enquiries. I just sailed in cheerfully on the first day of term. Now this happened to be January of the spring term – I had moved mid-year to seize the opportunity to work locally – and was taking over a Year 3 class of 7 to 8 year olds for two terms, with the agreement that I could move into establishing an all-age 'remedial' class in the next academic year.

This is how it went:

- There was a head, a deputy head and seven class teachers.
- The male head and the female deputy head were each about 100 years old.
- They had not spoken to each other for the past seven years after a disagreement.
- The deputy spoke to no one.
- The connecting door between my classroom and hers was kept locked from her side.
- The head was pleasant and courteous to all (other than his deputy) but contributed nothing.
- There was not one staff meeting in the one and a half years I was there.
- There was no professional development.
- The Year 5 and Year 6 teachers often did not come to the staffroom for days on end, they ate in their classrooms and talked together.
- The Year 4 teacher was strange and, having become a prison visitor at Wakefield Jail – a massive and fearsome high security establishment – was engaged to a murderer.
- Reception and Years 1 and 2 were in a separate building, so rarely seen.
- Year 3s are *small* and nothing I had learned in secondary was relevant or helpful.
- I had no mentor, and no one offered help.
- I was considered mature and experienced and I just had to get on with it.
- You can't talk to 7 year olds the way you talk to 14 year olds.
- 7 year olds can't concentrate for long inputs.
- 7 year olds can't sit still for long periods.
- 7 year olds can't work for long periods at one task.

I found that I could no longer 'plan' just three sessions a day with one activity filling each session. I needed to think in four to six sessions, with shifts in the type of activity within each session, although all sessions could be on the same aspect of learning. We still didn't 'do' true planning, just jotted ideas, or even sat on the front of our desks chatting to the children and waiting for inspiration to come. I also found it was full-on interaction for five and a half hours a day in the classroom. No more 'sneaky' ten minutes at my desk whilst the pupils painted or drew or modelled or worked clay or just generally messed about, depending on the class, as I had done at the secondary school.

The shifts within sessions included three or more changes of locality or activity for variety. The introduction to the lesson often took place with children seated on the carpet in a cluster while I set the scene for the learning, made clear what the expectation was by the end of the lesson and taught any new aspects of learning. This might have been followed by a demonstration or shared model of what was to be done. The class relocated to their tables and each produced the work required, or they worked in pairs, threes or small groups to produce the task.

The task may have been the completion of sums or problem solving. It may have been writing, drawing, making a model, painting or something similar. There was often a mini-plenary part way through the activity, to review what the task was and perhaps use some of the children's emerging work to demonstrate success. The children then continued and completed the work before the plenary, which may have been conducted with them gathered once again on the carpet. The outcomes were reviewed against the expectations from the introduction, with the sharing of one or two children's work in most cases. The lesson closed, usually with me giving a brief overview of where the learning would go next, and the work was collected in for marking if appropriate.

The above model is accepted practice today, but – with no prior experience and no help – I had to work it out for myself. It was the summer term before I could reap the rewards and really start enjoying having lots of riotous fun with my class, often with much laughter and much noise.

No one cared because no one came near me.

The summer term brought other enrichment. I discovered that on sunny days I could take my class out for nature walks, across the fields or down through the woods, collecting twigs and leaves, wildflowers, interesting stones and other wonders of nature. We would carry them back to school and look them up to make labels, placing them on the nature table – a very important part of the classroom. We would paint and draw these treasures in art or science.

There was no safeguarding in those days and certainly no risk assessment. I took the whole class by myself and they behaved beautifully, but I cringe now at the thought of what could have happened. We had no mobile phones... What would have happened if one of the children had fallen and hurt themselves, or even more likely, if I had? Sometimes we did these walks two or three times a week, and never even let the office know we were going out!

And no one ever seemed to notice...

Thank goodness it is different in primary schools today!

Today, many newly qualified teachers spend a year or more on supply teaching round various schools before achieving a permanent position. They do not usually have a mentor, and when placements are short, they may not have time to find their way through the learning process to experience the joy that teaching brings. This is not a satisfactory introduction to the profession, and the one piece of advice I would give them is not to make my fundamental mistake – make a friend or friends and ask them for advice.

My Top Tips for Radical Phase or School Moves

- Consider carefully what it is you want to achieve and how best you might do that.
- Talk to friends and colleagues in the profession.
- Research the age you will be teaching.
- Research (discreetly) the school you are applying to.
- Ask (politely) if you can visit the school to be shown round before interview.
- Smile at everyone you meet, but also show serious intent and interest through questions.
- Watch the children, how they behave, how they respond to each other and adults.
- Watch the teachers, how they interact with the children, how they articulate.
- Study wall displays (if time) – they represent creativity, achievement and variety.
- Study your journey, will it be too stressful?

CHAPTER 3

My First Five Years as a Teacher

Written by Kirstie Pilmer – a class teacher in her fifth year in the profession.

Introduction

I am currently in my fifth year of teaching after completing the ITT (Initial Teacher Training) programme over the 2014/2015 academic year. Before entering teaching, I worked as an events co-ordinator for an education company. Primarily, my role was to organise and manage conferences in hotels and support in-school INSET days. I was extremely lucky that part of the role was working with experienced teachers, headteachers and consultants. I travelled all around the UK speaking to and watching teachers talk about their craft. That's how I was introduced to Ros, who is now a dear friend. We worked closely together as we travelled up and down the country.

I had the pleasure of watching Ros impart her knowledge and experience to large crowds of teachers and I got to know her on a personal level. This helped me to get a far greater understanding of what it meant to be a teacher. I saw the formal part of teaching at the conferences and heard all of the stories (some with horror but mostly with humour) as we sat to eat dinner in hotels. I learned a lot, and it put me in a very good position to go into teaching. However, there was still a huge amount to learn. I had gained some insight into teaching but I still looked at the profession through rose tinted spectacles. Working as an events co-ordinator was stressful, so my dad and I often joked that I wouldn't know what stress was like after I started my new 8am to 3pm role. How naive I was!

The ITT Programme

The programme, as I experienced it, was only satisfactory. I was class-based four days a week with a day of training on a Friday. Fridays were such a treat. We sat in a room, drank lots of tea, ate lots of biscuits and just listened. It was a doddle! My training was very 'tick boxey' in my opinion; by that I mean we weren't taught anything ground breaking, it was just the basic safeguarding, Assessment for Learning (AfL), lesson planning and so on. I think we were supposed to learn all the exciting parts of teaching in school, however that was very dependent on the school you were placed in. The school I was in had been judged 'Requires Improvement' (RI) and was in an extremely deprived area. I learned a lot about behaviour management and parental engagement – because I had to. These were the two biggest problems the school faced but that meant other areas of my development were lacking. Looking back, I have nothing against the school, but I was not their main priority. They definitely had bigger fish to fry, shall we say. I bumbled my way through with the help of a good mentor and class teacher and I must not have done a bad job because they employed me for my NQT year.

Looking back on this time, I question whether the one-year programmes are enough. Is a year enough to go from (in my case) never setting foot in a classroom before to teaching your own class? No, is my honest answer. Four out of ten teachers leave in the first five years of teaching and I believe this is because they feel they are ill-equipped to do the job. They feel like they are failing when in fact they are still learning. I often wonder about the idea that a teacher who has trained for a year on the ITT, SKITT or PGCE courses can be as well-equipped as those who have studied three or four years on the BA honours programme. I also question whether schools who have had more than one RI inspection should take on students. If they are not meeting the standards expected of them, then how are they going to train future teachers to a high standard? It doesn't make sense. The only reason I can see is that we don't have enough schools that are good or outstanding to train the number of teachers that we need.

Top Tips for Initial Training

- Don't just rely on the training you are being given. Go out and improve yourself. Go on Twitter and immerse yourself in EduTwitter. Look for good practice and teaching ideas by doing lots of reading and talking to other teachers.
- If you get the choice of school, look carefully at their most recent Ofsted inspection. Just because a school is RI, it doesn't mean that you shouldn't go for it, but it will give you a good idea where it is currently on the continuum of improvement.
- Ask for the training you want. There's lots of good training online which is very cheap.
- Don't be afraid to tell your training provider you're not happy with the school if you feel like you are not getting the attention you deserve and need.

My NQT Year

Going into my NQT year, I really thought I knew what I was doing. My classroom looked fantastic (just as I have subsequently seen most other NQT's classrooms). On reflection, it was probably one of the only things I knew how to do and that was because I had mirrored the practice of the person who had the room before me. It was bright and engaging and my desk was lined with highlighters and coloured marking pens. I had all the gear and no idea, as the saying goes. The first few weeks were fantastic. It was me, my teaching assistant and my very own class. I felt like a superstar. The children were well behaved – as they always are in the beginning of an academic year – and I felt like I really had it in the bag.

My first real test was in my third week when, in the middle of a lesson, I heard the biggest scream. It came from one of my 'tougher' boys. He ran over to me with one pump on and the other in his hand, shouting 'Look Miss, look! He's spat in my shoe.' It was probably the strangest thing someone had ever said to me. I looked and there was a ball of phlegm sat on the inner-sole of the pump he was holding out to me. What do you say to that? Nobody told me how to handle this when I was attending my Friday training day. I did what any reasonable person would do and asked him to go and wash it off. Wash it he did. He was taking quite a while, so I went to see what was going on. As I entered the sink area, I found him holding his pump under the cold tap. It was overflowing with water and splashing all over his uniform. He looked at me, proud as punch, as I stared back. But that wasn't the worst of it...

Whilst he had been washing it, he had realised the water was filling up as it would in a cup. So, what did he do as I stood there looking at him? He drank from his pump. I was horrified. What kind of a person drinks out of a shoe? A shoe that had been spat in just 10 minutes prior. It was at that moment I learned the lesson of clear instruction. Had I been clear, the boy wouldn't have been filling his pump full of water or using it as a drinking vessel. Giving clear instructions wasn't all I learned during my NQT year. I learned how to coax children down from tables (who were leap frogging from one table to another); I learned how to stop angry parents from fighting with each other; but most significantly of all, I learned how to 'fake it' to the rest of the teaching staff.

Top Tips for Instructing Pupils

- When asking a child to do something, give very short and clear instructions.
- Never assume they know what you mean.
- Try to never show you are shocked by anything.

Teacher Types

My first school had quite a few of what I now call 'teacher types'. They are the colleagues who are allegedly the best teachers in the world. If they are to be believed, they never make mistakes and they always have outstanding lessons. In my first year, I became one of those. My first 'teacher type performance' came after one of the worst lessons of my career. We were learning about division. The children had started arguing about resources and a fight had ensued in my class. One child was hiding under a desk and the other was standing on top of it like a lion roaring from on top of a rock. I went to the staffroom for a well-deserved cup of tea and everyone was discussing their seemingly outstanding lessons.

Within minutes of entering the room, I found myself doing the same, when actually it had been the exact opposite. Every break and lunch time was the same. They all boasted and I joined in. It wasn't like me at all, but I felt like the only one who had bad lessons. I felt like a failure and I was scared to admit it. My mentor would tell me that I was doing a good job, but I thought she was just trying to make me feel good. I had never been in a job that was so analytical and self-critical. In my previous role, the only feedback I got was when things had either gone amazingly well or absolutely terribly. Teaching is one of the only jobs where you are constantly told how to improve. It was alien to me, and I thought that I was on my own and failing.

Fast forward five years and I know that nobody is perfect, nobody always has outstanding lessons (if any at all). We all have those lessons that you have planned for hours but two minutes in, you realise it isn't working and you have to scrap them. I also know that being able to share and reflect on your practice with your peers is the best form of development you can have. I often tell my current colleagues about lessons that have gone wrong and we discuss what I could have done differently. A lot of that is down to the school I am now in. In this school, we have an open staffroom where we can totally be ourselves. These colleagues were actually the ones that coined the phrase 'teacher types' because as a staff, that is exactly what we strive to avoid.

Top Tips for Settling into a Class
- Ask for help. If you know something hasn't gone well, ask how you could have improved it, or how others would have done it differently.
- Have the confidence to be open and honest about your lessons.
- Laugh about your mistakes. Everyone makes them and they can be quite humorous when you look back on them.

Moving Schools
After my NQT year, I made the decision to move schools. This wasn't for the reasons it should have been. I was working about 45 minutes from where I lived, and with the rush hour traffic, it was taking its toll. Working in a school

is mentally draining and there can be really long days, so with travel on top it was too much. Relocating was the best decision I've made but not just because of the travel time. I applied for three posts and I was lucky enough to get interviews for them all. My first interview was for another RI school. I said to myself that I didn't want the job because I wanted a school that could really invest their time in me, but it would be good interview practice for the other two (good) schools. This changed the moment I set foot into the first school. The staff were welcoming, one sang to me and another joked that I was too good looking to work in the school. I immediately felt at home and not just because of the 'good looking' comment.

The headteacher showed me around the school and I made the odd remark about the things that I was seeing and talked to a few children. She gave nothing away. I was led to a small room where the other candidates were sitting. My interview was first then I had a 20-minute lesson observation with a Year 1 class. I was dreading the interview. It was with a governor and the deputy headteacher in a tiny room. They took it in turns to ask me questions, most of which I had practised the night before (if you Google 'teaching interview questions', a long list comes up). I also took a folder which was really useful. If I found myself temporarily 'stuck' for things to say, I could show examples of what I had done in the past or show evidence to back up what I was saying.

I came out beaming and thinking that I had done the best that I possibly could. I'd managed to answer all of the questions and because of the practice, I had a lot to say. I went back to the room where the other candidates were sitting and had just sat down when the headteacher walked into the room we were all in and said 'I'm not interested in the interview, it's the lesson that needs to be good.' My heart dropped. I was petrified. But she was right, the interview is there to give them an idea of who you are, but good teaching is the key.

When it was time for my lesson, I was taken to the classroom and left with 30 Year 1 children. I didn't get a chance to set up, it was just me and a class full of children I'd never met with two very important people judging me. I think this is the point where you either sink or swim. That is when a vital piece of Ros's advice came back to me, 'fake it until you make it' and it's so true in teaching. I turned from being a scared little girl into a confident teacher.

I am not the most confident person in everyday life, and I don't like the attention being on me. In teaching, I have found that you need to pretend to be confident even when you're not. If not, the children pick up on it and that's when negative behaviour starts.

Whilst I set up my screens, I started counting so the children weren't just sat there. I counted to 100 from different starting points because I knew that was an objective they were working on. This is something I had learned at my previous school, keep children busy and it will keep them out of trouble. For the lesson, I had prepared number bonds to ten work and after questioning the children for a couple of minutes, I realised that quite a few children already knew them. I quickly moved the children who were already confident onto reasoning and problem-solving questions so that they were appropriately challenged. This showed that I could adapt and think on my feet. I had also prepared lots of practical resources for the children who found number bonds tricky, which showed I understood how to differentiate using concrete apparatus. It wasn't the best lesson I've ever taught but, whilst I was in the room, I made sure the children were engaged and challenged appropriately.

As the deputy led me back to the 'waiting' room, I made sure that I reflected on my practice, I told her what had gone wrong even though she pretended she wasn't listening. We haven't discussed it since, but I know her well enough now to know she was listening. It is important to note here too; the lesson went much better because I had telephoned ahead. I asked every important question I could think of, things like: how many children will there be? Will there be any extra adults in the room? Are there any children who are on the SEND register? If so, what are their needs? What topics have they been learning about? I should have also asked roughly how many are at the expected standard because then maybe I would have known they knew their number bonds to ten. I also asked about equipment to make sure I would have an interactive whiteboard (one of the schools didn't, so that is worth bearing in mind).

Top Tips for Attending Interviews

- Be prepared for the interview: take folders with pictures of displays, reports from training, lesson observations (the good ones).
- Be prepared for your lesson: have any printed material in wallets so you can quickly pass them around the tables, take any practical equipment with you, think of some good activities the children can be doing whilst you are setting up, like counting.
- Question the children to get a good grasp on what they can already do so you can differentiate the rest of the lesson accordingly.
- Ring the school before hand to ask for abilities, topics studied, SEND.
- Fake it in the classroom. Be the most confident person you can be.
- If possible, reflect on the lesson with someone who has observed you. This shows that you want to improve and be a better teacher.

I Got the Job!

The school was rated 'Requires Improvement' by Ofsted, but it was a dramatically improving school. It was the polar opposite to the one I had been in previously. The leadership team were a strong unit and they had a clear plan of how to turn the school around.

I worked for two years with an amazing and very experienced teacher who is now a good friend. I learned a lot. I actually learned how to teach, at long last. We laughed together and quite often cried together. We were both in Year 2 (the school is two-form entry). I didn't mind the stress of a SATs year too much but it was definitely a stress. I always remember, as Christmas approached, thinking, 'how on earth are these children going to be at the expected level?' but somehow we got them there. We planned together and always talked about how the lessons had gone. Because I was in my RQT year, I got the opportunity to observe her and other experienced teachers, which is a treat you never have, the further in your career you progress, until you move into management.

I was moved to Year 3 after two years. I was pleased at first because I had only briefly worked in Key Stage 2 before. I realised very quickly that my colleague from Year 2 had been amazing but maybe a little too amazing.

I had unknowingly relied on her and passed all decisions by her, so when I was put with a new year group partner, who I didn't have that relationship with, it was tough. Added to this, I had a very difficult class. There were many children with very challenging behaviour and several children had SEND with no 1:1 support. I found the challenging behaviours stemmed from two children and when they started to misbehave the rest of the class did too. When I got one of them on board, the other one disobeyed everything I said because they wanted the attention. It was a constant battle to try to get them in line, some days I would win, and the class would be good fun, but other days would be an absolute nightmare and I would feel completely out of control. As a teacher, feeling out of control is the worst feeling you can have. I felt like a failure when I called for support from management, but I had to because the situation was becoming quite unsafe.

I spent most of that fourth year with an awful anxious feeling in the pit of my stomach, feeling that I had done something wrong. There were many reasons for this. One was that we had 'drop-ins' instead of formal observations. They were 10- to 20-minutes long and they could happen at any time. In Year 2, they hadn't bothered me as much but because my new class were very unpredictable, I absolutely dreaded them. My tummy used to do a somersault every time I heard the door go or if I used to see a member of leadership walk by with the 'dreaded clipboard'. They always seemed to walk in when someone was just tipping a pot of counters onto the floor or throwing something across the room. The worst part was that I didn't have the confidence to react in the way I usually would. I would freeze and it would look like I was out of control. I also struggled to juggle all the jobs I needed to. I would find myself marking for hours so it would get to eight o'clock in the evening and I would have nothing planned for the next day. This led to rushed lesson planning and not great outcomes. I was stuck in a vicious cycle where I hated my job. I felt like I was failing myself and more importantly the children.

It all came to a head when, one morning, I sat at my desk and cried. I was dreading the children coming in. All I wanted to do was run out of the building and never come back. I didn't though. This was the career I had wanted my whole life, and I enjoyed every year except this one. I went to the toilet, washed my face and acted the life out of that day. I look back now and believe it was genuinely the best day of my career so far. The children were exactly the same, but my attitude had completely changed.

I started to realise that the 'drop-ins' weren't the be all and end all of teaching. I had been so tightly wound up and focused on these that it had consumed so much of my energy, when I should have been more focused on the children's progress and learning. I learned, with the help of my colleagues, to prioritise. One colleague gave me some of the best advice, she said always ask yourself why. Why are you marking all the books? Why are you differentiating three ways? Why do all your SEND have 'now and next' cards? If the answer is a legitimate one then do it, but if it's 'because we've been asked to' or 'because I've always done it this way' then don't, because as long as you can justify your actions then you'll be fine, in most cases. I say 'in most cases' because teaching sometimes feels like you are ticking boxes for the sake of it, but you need to know which ones need to be done and that's something that is key to figure out in your first few years of teaching.

From that day, I stopped marking for the sake of it, I stopped differentiating my lessons three ways if it wasn't needed and I stopped with all the 'now and next' cards (for the children who didn't need them). Nobody noticed. Nobody came to me and asked why it wasn't being done. It allowed me to be more creative and enjoy planning and teaching lessons. The children made more progress in that term than they ever had. We became absorbed in a deforestation topic and planned how we were going to change the world. We debated (something the challenging children were brilliant at), we campaigned, we wrote letters to the headteacher and we even set up a deforestation afterschool club to plan our next steps. It became a term I will never forget; the term that defined my teaching career. It was in this term that I truly became a teacher.

Top Tips for Maturing as a Teacher

- Prioritise: you can't do everything, so make sure you do the important jobs first. If you don't change a display for half a term, does it really matter?
- If you are not sure which jobs to prioritise, ask someone with more experience.
- Always ask yourself why. If you don't think it's important, then don't do it.
- Enjoy what you do. If you are enthusiastic about what you are teaching, then the children will be enthusiastic about learning.
- Talk to your colleagues (this is something I found really tough); ask them for advice and have a cup of tea and talk about your problems.

Conclusions

I have just finished my fifth year of teaching and it was a completely different experience. I was confident in my 'teacher skin' for the first time. When I worked with Ros, she always told me that it takes five years to become a teacher but I never understood what she meant. It is so hard to describe, but it feels as though someone just flicked a switch and suddenly I got it. Things I wasn't sure about previously slotted into place, and now I feel like I can see the whole picture rather than lots of little parts of it. I'm definitely not the perfect teacher, far from it, but I know I am doing the best for the children I teach. The job is really tough, and I still never feel like I have enough hours in the day, but now I am truly enjoying the teaching profession and I am enjoying the amazing children I teach.

CHAPTER 4

Returning to Teaching

I have never left teaching; I have been in the profession all my adult life – 55 years at the time of writing this book. However, I did return to England after almost 17 years in and around the Caribbean and, from discussions with others, I gather my experience of returning to England after 17 years was very similar to that of many teachers who return to the profession after a career break. So much had changed in education in England whilst I was overseas.

The final seven years of my first time overseas were spent on a tiny island 12 miles long and one mile wide with three small primary schools and one secondary school. Everyone knew everyone and life was close to idyllic – if you don't suffer from claustrophobia! There was no imposed curriculum, no testing, no external accountability. A school was as good as its head and staff, and the heads of the very small primary schools taught full-time so had little opportunity to observe or monitor.

Fortunately, my experiences there were all positive, with conscientious teachers teaching the many aspects of the curriculum they knew best and felt passion for, and the children mainly made very good progress. Sadly, my return to England with my two young teen children was a move I had not anticipated and had not planned, but I arrived back at Heathrow on the 27th September 1986 with no home, no job, no car and no networks other than family, obliged to restart my life in England.

Moving back up to Yorkshire, my home county, was an easy decision as life was more affordable in the north than in Surrey, where we spent the first two weeks back. The family all rallied round and my in-laws were marvellous. In fact, it was my sister-in-law who was responsible for finding me my first post within three weeks of my return as she had a close friend who was having three months off work for surgery, and the school needed a long term supply teacher – positions few and far between at that time.

Bearing in mind that I am predominantly an English and art primary specialist, the supply cover was in a very large comprehensive school on the edge of Leeds, and was to specialise in maths and science! I was assured, however, that there were full-time lab technicians with me for the science lessons and that they would set all the experiments up and even conduct them for me if I wished. Thus it was that I built a wardrobe of autumn and winter clothing through trips round the charity shops, and headed off to my new role in the beautiful, second-hand Hyundai car my brother-in-law had helped me to purchase.

All my classes were fine, except one Year 10 class, stream eight of nine. Luckily, the low ability range of the group meant that the maths itself was within my capabilities, but the behaviour and motivation of the group was appalling. I had not had to worry about discipline in the Caribbean, I was teaching what I loved to pupils I grew to love, who had parents who supported the schools implicitly and valued their children's education. Now I had a group who clearly hated maths and anyone who tried to inflict it on them, knew I was a supply teacher and thus fair game, and didn't care whether they learned or not.

As I attempted to arouse enthusiasm in the class for graphs, problem solving and measures, they shouted inane comments – mainly to or at me, but also at each other. The core three disrupters would mock anyone who appeared to be trying too hard, and rarely completed any work I set. Unfortunately I was not in a good place myself, due to the breakup of my marriage and the enforced return to Yorkshire, and thus was unable, for most of the time, to apply the principles of positivity, confidence, warmth and that much-needed smile. My body language was wrong, my facial expressions were wrong and my verbal reactions were negative. I felt I was failing that group and I did not know how to redeem it.

Of course, if you don't get on top of mutiny in the early days, each passing week makes it less and less likely that you ever will with that particular group – and I never did. I was in that school for two months and my other three science classes were making great strides – as was my second year maths group – but 10.8 appeared to have gone nowhere, and every session (four days a week) was a tense battle of wills.

It was like a miracle when I saw a job in the Times Educational Supplement for an English specialist in a middle school in Bradford. The journey would be much harder, but the age and ethos were perfect for me. I applied and was successful, being due to start in the January.

When I went to inform the deputy for curriculum that I would be leaving the Leeds school at the close of the term he was clearly shocked, and informed me that they had been so pleased with my work, and with the reports from the two heads of department and the technical staff, that they were intending to offer me a permanent post! I was bemused. I had never met the heads of either department and had no idea that anyone had ever even registered my existence, let alone noticed what I was doing. And you should have seen my face when the deputy then added:
'And the way you managed 10.8 was remarkable, I usually have a constant stream of miscreants outside my office from that lot!'

The worst part of my return to teaching in England, however, was the loneliness and isolation, which I had not felt in a school since completing my first years in England. The very large staffroom had clusters of comfortable armchairs arranged in circles and ovals around low tables, and the staff all seemed to sit in the same seats every break and every lunch time. It was so reminiscent of Normanton Secondary Modern School 18 years earlier. Just inside the main door into the staffroom, there were five upright chairs arranged in a straight line with their backs to the wall, and when I first arrived the deputy had indicated these five chairs and advised me that they were the 'supply chairs' for the supply staff. I had spent every single break and lunch perched, usually alone, on one of these chairs, clutching a mug of coffee and desperately trying not to look like a 'Billy-No-Mates', which I was.

Nobody spoke to me, nobody smiled at me. I did not exist, and I spoke to no one, and smiled at no one and strove desperately not to make eye contact. And at night I went home and cried. I suspect all my defence barriers were up, my body language was negative, and I was subconsciously holding others at arm's length. I could have sought out the heads of department, I could have consulted the head of fourth year about 10.8, I could have smiled and said 'good morning' to colleagues – but I did not. I withdrew and became Mrs Nobody, sitting with my back to the wall on a metal supply chair.

If I had been in a state to follow my own and others' top tips, perhaps things would have been different. That school further damaged an already damaged woman – don't let that happen to you. I would have been better off working in Marks and Spencer for a month or two until I 'recovered', rather than enduring the isolation and the soul-destroying behaviour of 10.8.

My Top Tips for Returning to Teaching

- Don't return to work unless you are fully recovered from whatever caused your absence.
- Don't return to work unless you are in the right frame of mind – or are confident you can fake it!
- Seek people out, make connections, smile and make eye contact.
- Smile and say 'good morning' to people.
- Ask for advice or help if you need it.
- If you have to, 'fake it to make it'.

CHAPTER 5

Fake it to Make It...

Those first five years of professional (and, more often than not, non-professional) experience taught me my biggest tip for teachers new to teaching or new to a phase or type of school.

You need to 'fake it to make it'!

I have always been a bit of a thespian and at one point it was a close call whether I tried for commercial art or the stage. Now I see I wouldn't have been good enough for either – but maybe as a sometimes comedienne... Who knows? And to be honest, I have had such a wonderful, rich life through education that I have no regrets.

In the face of my perceived early failure when I joined the profession, I started watching the other teachers around me, especially the 'cool' teachers, the confident teachers, the highly respected teachers and the popular teachers. Today, all newly qualified teachers hone their classroom skills through observation; we didn't have that opportunity when I first entered the classroom, but here I am recommending observation for presence and demeanour. I listened to the pupils as they chatted during art, and could soon have drawn up a list of the staff that the students held in high regard – and the ones they didn't. I watched teachers' demeanours as they moved through the school day, their interaction with pupils and other adults – and the over-all image they portrayed. The ones I personally admired were very different from each other, and none of them were me, but I learned something from all of them and customised it into my own personal image over those first years. This is a slow process, and one of the main reasons why it can take up to five years to become a teacher.

I need to say that all my role models for 'teacher image' were in the secondary school; there were none during my first experience of primary teaching, but I have had the privilege of observing so many wonderful teachers in primary schools since then that I know that was just an indictment of my first primary experience.

Analysing the elements of effective image may be a skill we do not all have. It is a little like the fact that I was a fairly effective PE teacher and a highly effective swimming coach who, in another part of my life, enabled schools to bring home many accolades and trophies, which will highly amuse the many of you who know me well. Of course, I wasn't always large, but I was certainly far from nimble – and 'athletic' or 'sporting' or 'mermaid' were certainly terms that would never be applied to me. However, I did have the ability to watch those who were effective, and analyse what it was they did, or had, that made them different, and then to convey that in words to pupils as they practised and trained.

Those were, therefore, the skills I deployed to improve my own effectiveness and image as a teacher.

The following is a synopsis:
- Image: clothing, hair and jewellery.
- Image: stance, bearing and walk.
- Attitude: positivity, mood and response to others.
- Attitude: body language.
- Confidence: in class and around school.

As soon as I had identified these features as ones I admired and needed to improve, I started 'copying' them. I never practised them out of context, but I developed another new skill that I call, 'The Robbie Burns Skill':

To a Louse, On Seeing One on a Lady's Bonnet at Church (1786)

'Oh, would some power the gift to gee us,
To see ourselves as others see us.'
(Translation from the Scottish, so forms may vary)

I have developed, when needed, the ability to 'see' myself as others might be seeing me – as I teach, move around a building, or even present to my peers, parents or others. This does not enable me to 'see' my facial expressions, and I have often been horrified at what the camera does to the sweet and angelic expressions and smiles I believe I am presenting. Nor does it explain why my gentle, dulcet tones are transformed into a raucous, broad Yorkshire accent by the microphone, but it does give me a fairly accurate picture of body language, stance and appearance of confidence that has so helped me over the many years.

1. Image

Clothing, Hair and Jewellery

The style and preference of your clothing is always your choice. However, I would strongly recommend that you do re-examine your own image periodically and ask yourself where you developed your style choices and for what settings. I didn't 'develop' style choices consciously in my teens and student years; rather I erred towards the culture of the 'hippy' of the '60s. Not too extreme – but to the comfortable, the convenient for the job and the economical. Give me two pairs of jeans and three big, baggy, black sweaters and I can still exist happily today (and continue to do so at home!)

Having 'examined' your appearance as a *teacher* rather than a student, you make choices. What you choose to do, even if it is nothing, is fine as long as it works for you, is acceptable to the school (some have strong dress codes which must be followed or you shouldn't be there) and will not possibly affect your ability to build a rapport with your pupils. For example, I made a conscious decision not to change my hair, which was long and thick, even though, on a staff of 50 plus, I was the only one without a more conformist style. It remained that way until I was in my forties!

When I entered the profession, I was still dressed much in my college style. It was 'The Robbie Burns Skill' that led to a gradual shift towards a slightly softer and more professional look. Not drastically – I still wore baggy sweaters in winter, but I did acquire two or three smarter skirts (albeit cheap from C&A – the Primark of the era) and several nice tops.

I repeated the process as I moved through the profession, so that by the time I was entering senior leadership and then advisory work, I was never without a professional jacket – and I still find it very hard to be without one today when I am working. I have always said that when the jacket goes on the head goes up and the eyes light up. Game on!

Stance, Bearing and Walk

It would be easy to say that this is only your business, that you are an adult and that patterns are now established – and all those things are true. However, watch those around you whom you admire or you consider command respect. Consider how the way they carry themselves around school complements their image or not. Watch as they talk to colleagues, to pupils and to others in school. Watch them at the front of their classes (I had to resort to peeping through the glass panels in doors or corridor windows, as we were given no opportunities to observe in classrooms in the 1960s).

Note their confidence, their purposefulness, and their alertness to the responses (verbal and non-verbal) of their pupils. Reflect and use your 'Robbie Burns Skill' to 'watch' yourself… this is not a 'practise in front of a mirror' job; it means hover above yourself in your mind's eye as you teach, slightly to your front, and be aware of how confident, mobile and aware you seem to the class. These factors help to encourage discipline, engagement, and alertness in learners.

2. Attitude

Positivity, Mood and Response to Others

We can't all always be cheerful, feel well, have no problems in our lives and be eternally positive, but there is no doubt that these are all factors that can alter both mood and attitudes to teaching.

Everyone has good lessons and not so good lessons, good days and not so good days, and if we are totally honest, most of us had some very poor lessons and very poor days when we first started to teach (and very occasionally throughout our careers). I know I did. In the beginning it is usually because we have not yet fully developed the skills of teaching, of engaging pupils, managing their attitudes and behaviours and motivating them – all while delivering content and challenge appropriate to the point we are at in the curriculum.

However, we soon become aware that our most effective days are the days when our mood is positive, when we are feeling good about ourselves and our pupils and when we are teaching something we know well and care about and understand it is important to the class.

When we have the privilege of watching highly effective teachers, we see they radiate these qualities with positivity, passion and a huge belief in their pupils' ability to learn. None of us started out that way in the beginning, or – if we did – we soon found the reality. However, we can all 'fake it to make it', and if we fake it well enough for long enough it becomes natural to us – a newly established professional persona.

Leave the personal baggage at the classroom door – it will only get in the way of your teaching.

Lift the chin, put a smile on your face and sweep into your room. It takes practice to maintain it, to keep praising the positives and ignoring, as far as possible, the negatives, but it will come! If you don't aim for it – it may not come.

Conduct your classes like an orchestra: sweep them up into highs and soothe them back down into calm and quiet.

Body Language

In 1992, the entire team of advisors at Kirklees Local Authority were given professional training in presentation skills by an external specialist consultancy. It was a full week and we were all videoed, presenting on a ten-minute theme on the first day, so that we could identify the areas where we needed to improve. We also viewed each other's videos and identified three positives and two areas for improvement. We were then filmed again on a new theme on the last day, following three days of coaching and observation, so that we could identify our own improvement. I learned so much from that process, and from the practise and input we received in the three days between.

The following are skills I have honed and developed intentionally as a result of that experience:

- Too much 'clutter' in clothing and accessories can be a distraction, for example highly patterned or colourful scarves, lots of big, bold jewellery, lots of piercings, elaborate hair decorations, etc. This does not mean you shouldn't wear these things, just be aware.

- Moments of complete stillness help when making crucial points for emphasis: stand very still and full face, feet a few inches apart and arms loosely at your sides and make eye contact. Leaning very slightly forward adds emphasis.

- Moving around whilst doing oral input is good, as long as it is bold, confident and deliberate. Frenetic movement can cause anxiety and distraction.

- Arm and hand gestures should also be bold and deliberate. 'Flapping' is a distraction.

- Use pause and suspense deliberately in oral input when appropriate. Either maintain eye contact or deliberately turn away for a moment. Even look back over one shoulder, and then perhaps you could swing round to finish the point.

- Vary your voice pitch and tone as you deliver input, sometimes exuding lively enthusiasm and sometimes using a softer, more measured tone.

- Be conscious of your stance – as said before – mainly stand tall, chin up, eye contact, bright eyes, slight smile if appropriate and a large, bold gesture when gesture is appropriate.

3. Confidence

In Class and Around School

This is one of the biggest 'fakes' for many of us in the early days. Please remember that a) practice makes perfect and b) tomorrow is another day!

- Stand straight and 'walk tall'.
- Chin up slightly.
- Shoulders back and down.
- Make eye contact with people as you pass.

- Smile slightly as often as possible or as is appropriate.
- Greet colleagues warmly and confidently, even though you may not know them well yet.
- Be firm but fair with children.
- Keep calm and carry on.
- Meet and greet classes at the classroom door.
- Greet pupils warmly, including the more challenging ones.
- Tell pupils that a light touch on the back of the shoulder means you are thinking of them even if you haven't actually spoken to them. Use it as you move around the room.
- Volunteer for small jobs as long as you feel confident, and they will not increase your stress.

Very little of all the above comes naturally for most of us. I have been learning and faking all my life – and still am. When I am at conferences, I watch other presenters and identify any especially effective techniques I could embrace, and then I use my 'Robbie Burns Skill' of hovering and watching myself to see how they sit with me.

I always end up adapting and modifying to suit my personal delivery and content, but if any tweak improves communication or impact, that is good in my book! So, please remember, in the beginning we all need to '*fake it to make it*'!

My Top Tips for Establishing a Persona as a Teacher

- Be aware of the image you are portraying.
- Watch the demeanour of those you admire as they move around the school and interact with others.
- Adopt and adapt strategies you admire.
- Move with confidence, head held high.
- Greet people as you pass.
- Make eye contact.
- Smile.
- If you fake it well it will become real.

CHAPTER 6

Bribery and Penalties

In the teaching profession, bribery is called incentives and rewards. Whether it is stickers or sweets, 'golden time' or 'choosing time', the effect is the same as bribery:

'If you are good, you will get...'

'If you are not good, we won't have...'

Some don't agree with the practice, but there are not many in the profession who don't use incentives at some point in the week.

Bribery is intrinsic to human life. Parents use it all the time to persuade children to do something. They also use penalties or the withdrawal of privileges to persuade children not to do something. Whether it is going to the park or not going to the park, the playground or no playground, extra TV or no TV, extra technology time or no technology, sweets or no sweets – whatever the offering, it is still bribery and penalties.

It is the same in adulthood, many businesses pay bonuses as incentives to work harder or faster. Certain shops and stores have free this and low cost that to incentivise their staff. One large store even provided hair dressing and make up for their shop floor staff – a double bonus as the staff presented better and felt good about themselves.

Whatever you select as your main form of bribery, you must feel comfortable with it. Don't choose sweets if you feel you need to be furtive about them. Praise, when handled in the right way, is as good as a bag of fruit sweets. Children love to be praised and many children don't get enough praise in other parts of their lives. Research conducted in the USA found that middle class children received seven notes of praise from parents or teachers for every single negative comment, whereas poorer children received seven criticisms for every single positive comment.

Empty praise is meaningless. Look for good reasons to praise and give the reason you are pleased with the child. Ask yourself whether there is any child you can't remember praising recently. Every child does something well or right in a day, the trouble is we notice the negatives and, as teachers, we may focus on the negatives too much. If some children are slow to settle to their work, praise those who are already getting on with theirs. If someone is running on the corridor, praise all the ones who are walking smartly. You will be surprised how many will fall into line if you use praise as an incentive, because everyone wants to be praised.

Of course, if you start out with sweets it is very difficult to replace them with praise. Praise is then devalued so that it is no longer seen as something worth having. If you feel that pupils need a reward as well, you could give the reward as they are leaving class at the end of the day, or at break time or lunch time or even on Friday afternoons. Of course, if you are a secondary teacher you may not have that option. If you only see a class or group twice a week, the reward needs to be given by the second session at latest.

There are some pupils who are embarrassed by public praise, feeling it does not fit with the image they are trying to portray. Having a quiet word of praise as the student leaves the room can be as effective as public praise. Make pupils believe in themselves, give them confidence and the incentive to strive for learning. When I was an advisor for Kirklees Local Authority we had a team day with all 60 advisors and inspectors together. The head of service told us the following story:

When he was at secondary school (he named the school and it was one we all knew well in a more 'run down' large estate in Huddersfield), the class had an excessively grumpy science and maths teacher. I shall call him Mr Grump for the purposes of this publication.

One day, at the end of a science lesson, Mr Grump bellowed across the classroom, 'Granger, stay back after class please,' so he did. When all the other students had gone, Mr Grump stood and looked him over for a while and then said:

'Granger, I want you to know that you are a very foolish young man. You have a real talent for science and if you only worked harder you could go to one of the top universities in the country and become a highly successful scientist. You are equally capable at maths as well, in fact you are possibly the most talented student I have ever taught science and maths to.'

Our head of service told us that he couldn't get these words out of his head and, as a consequence, he started to pay more attention in his science lessons and his maths lessons and he found that he did indeed enjoy them and that he found both subjects fascinating, becoming very good at them. He got top marks in A-levels and he went on to university to study maths. He became a maths teacher, then head of department, then an inspector and finally our head of service.

Mr Granger married his girlfriend, who he had met while in the sixth form, and they both kept in touch with all their friends from school. One night, they decided to have a reunion and invited eight of their closest friends to dinner. Halfway through the meal, Mr Granger – for some reason unbeknown to himself – decided to tell the whole group what Mr Grump had said to him all those years ago.

One after another, spoons and forks clattered onto plates as his wife and friends stared at him in disbelief.

'But that's what Grump said to me one day too,' gasped his wife.

'And me...'

'He said it to me too...'

And soon it transpired that Mr Grump had picked off every single student in the group and told them quietly and in confidence that they were possibly the most talented student he had ever taught, and from that day every single student had started to work harder and take an interest and had ended up going to university or college and, as a result, enjoyed successful careers.

Such is the power and importance of self-belief!

One of the most successful strategies for incentives and rewards is classroom and curricular organisation. In my last three years in a primary school in Kirklees, before I joined the advisory team in 1992, I developed a system with my classes that I called 'The Menu System'. Two or three times a day (after registration, after break and after lunch), I did a taught input, explained the activity with great care and then put the title of the activity on the 'menu' which filled one of my two blackboards. Beneath the title of the activity was the date it had to be completed by. The rest of the time the class were free to work through the 'menu' in any order they wished. Some did the things they liked best first, and some chose to do the things they liked least first and then to luxuriate in their pleasures.

They all knew they could stop one activity and change to a different one whenever they felt the need, as long as all the items on the 'menu' for completion that week were finished by Friday lunch time. Friday afternoons were 'desserts' or 'tasty bits' that I would plan with great care as they were the treats that didn't often happen in school. There were always three to choose from, usually an educational video, an IT activity and an artistic activity.

The whole class knew that they would not get to do the 'tasty bits' if they hadn't completed all the tasks on the 'menu'. Because Friday afternoons became so popular, some children would ask if they might take unfinished work home to complete on Thursday nights, rather than miss out on 'dessert'. At the end of each day, completed work was placed on my desk for me to mark and 'sign off' if completed satisfactorily. Immediately after lunch on Fridays, I would call out the items from the 'menu' that had to be finished and the class would hold up their book or paper to show the distinctive 'signing off' that was angled, diagonally, across the corner of the page to indicate that I had accepted it as satisfactorily completed.

The art was to leave a few items on the 'menu' each weekend so that there was always something to start the next week's 'menu' off. There were never any discipline problems in these classes, no one was ever bored – they could just change activity if they had had enough – and no one wanted to miss Friday afternoons. The one thing no one was allowed to do was nothing! It was a structure that worked for the many challenged and challenging children in Year 6 from one of the most deprived estates in Kirklees. The only subjects not listed on the 'menu' were PE and music (the latter being taught by a specialist and the former being dictated by hall, playground, or field time – according to the season).

When two of the local authority inspectors, including the senior primary inspector, came in to observe my teaching because they had heard I had knowledge of assessment which most teachers did not have at that time, they were absolutely amazed to see these deprived children bustling around busily, self-resourcing and settling to work with no apparent supervision from me whilst I held a conversation with the visitors. Of course, I was covertly keeping a careful eye on things in reality as squabbles could flare up at any time – as they do in crowded classrooms.

My Top Tips for Incentives and Rewards

- Don't be afraid to use them.
- Don't promise something you are not going to fulfil.
- Make pupils believe in themselves and their abilities.
- Give pupils confidence and a thirst for learning.
- Use the carrot not the stick.
- Praise more often than you criticise.
- Make learning enjoyable and rewarding.
- Empower pupils with choice and time management as a powerful reward.

CHAPTER 7

Aspire to Inspire

Self-evaluation is a very important tool for a teacher, and it is not always used well enough. The profession has come to rely on observation by others to glean feedback, but being able to self-evaluate is an important part of the equation.

I always kept a little notebook in my handbag, with each page divided into five boxes for the four or five lessons of the day. At the end of the day I would have a period of quiet reflection, I would mark the books or other work given in, and I would score myself out of five for the effectiveness of each lesson. I don't think I ever gave myself fives, but I was very pleased when I felt a lesson deserved a four. Three was average and below three was unsatisfactory and I had to make a note of why I felt that. Thankfully, I did not give myself many ones or twos. At the end of the week, I would run a quiz to see how much of the key learning the children had retained. Of course, it was a 'beat your own last score' quiz, not a whole class competitive one.

Slowly a pattern would emerge in my scoring, with the subjects I knew well and loved scoring consistently higher than those I was less confident in. Design and technology was stubbornly a three, or even the rarer two, as was shape and space in maths, which I could never see the point of, but my beloved art, English, history, environmental geography, animal and botanical science all scored much more highly – as did PE, the four operations in maths and data handling.

The truth was there in the notebook – where I was not scoring well in my teaching, I did not have the same passion for the subject, and I didn't have the passion because I either did not have deep enough subject knowledge or I did not value the content enough.

This was information I would never get from a lesson observation, as I was too good at 'faking it to make it' if a visitor walked through the door. I now knew when I was firing up the class with my passion, when I was conducting them like an orchestra and when I was sweeping them along on a tide of excitement – and I knew how to convey that even when I did not truly feel it.

Having identified my areas of weakness, it was incumbent upon me to do something about it. Ideally, I would search the Kirklees news to see if there were courses running on the subject. Failing that, I would consult the subject co-ordinator – to see if they knew any more than I did. Sadly, subject leadership is too often a matter of inheritance rather than being the best person for the job. Can you believe I was leading on design and technology at the time? No one to consult there then...

Failing all else I would buy a book, or – if I was lucky – persuade the head to buy one for me. Sadly, the quality of books is very variable and many a book went on the staffroom bookshelves, unfinished due to disappointment. Then I would resort to that which I should have done in the first place – asking around the staff, visiting classrooms to see what their children had done or made. Sadly, in the case of design and technology, it was such a new subject that no one seemed to understand it any better than I did – nor seemed to care.

Inspirational Teaching

As an AST assessor (advanced skills teachers), it was necessary to be able to determine the difference between a very good teacher and an outstanding teacher. Of course, teachers had to be recommended by their headteachers and it was very sad, and deeply worrying, on the rare occasions when a teacher who was only mediocre was recommended. The implication was that this teacher was the best that the head had seen, and it happened infrequently, but when it did happen it was usually in a tiny number of rural schools.

I only 'passed' one such mediocre teacher and I have regretted it deeply ever since. Her headteacher was so full of praise and excitement for her, but the lesson was punctuated by a resounding thunderstorm and the pupils' behaviour was distracted and not good. In my heart I knew that an outstanding teacher should have been able to maintain the attention of their class – and perhaps even used the storm as a focus for diversion, to talk about what causes the thunder and the lightning – but she didn't and for some reason I bottled it and gave her the status. I have never forgiven myself for that because she was not outstanding, and I was cheapening the status of being an AST.

It was once again our head of service at Kirklees who set me thinking about inspirational teaching. He has a lot to answer for! He asked us all to mentally identify the most inspirational teacher who taught us, whether in primary or secondary school. Every one of the 60 of us succeeded – except me. I could not identify one teacher I found to be inspirational. How very sad after 14 years of being educated.

The team then identified the qualities of that teacher's teaching that they found to be inspirational – and it was life changing. After quiet reflection on those qualities, we shared them in small groups and were amazed how similar our thoughts were. No one listed 'knew more about maths than any other teacher I ever met' – or history or art. They listed generic qualities such as passion, humour, belief in pupils, entertaining, willing to go off-subject, anecdotal and so on. From our group discussions, we fed back the range of qualities and they were recorded on a flip chart. We were then asked to reflect on when we came closest to delivering those qualities in our own teaching.

This was life changing for me. It led me to identify when I was closest to being that inspirational teacher and – sure enough – it was when I was teaching the subjects I was passionate about, and definitely not when I was teaching the subjects I valued little or knew little about. This knowledge worked well with my 'Robbie Burns Skill' – I was able to float above myself and watch myself and evaluate when I was getting closest to being the inspirational teacher.

Now I could apply that knowledge to my 'fake it to make it' skills, and 'turn on' my passion and humour, even when teaching something I did not personally find inspirational. What an asset this proved to be. And I discovered that, even if I did not feel passion for the subject, I did for my pupils, and they – in their own often grey worlds – deserved the best, so I did my best... for them. And it usually worked, I am so pleased to say.

Sometimes it is purely a case of a teacher not having had the opportunity to teach children of the age that would be best for them. We tend – as teachers – to stay in the same phase or age group, even as we change schools. Consider requesting a transfer to an older or younger section of the school if you feel disaffected or unsure where your best talents lie, but ideally not after less than two years in one year group.

My Top Tips for Aspiring to Be Inspiring

- Improve your subject knowledge so that you can divert and follow the lead of the class when appropriate.
- Be flexible and listen to the class.
- Arouse passion in yourself to arouse passion in your pupils.
- Convey excitement and joy in the learning.
- Use humour consciously and effectively.
- Enrich your teaching with anecdotes when appropriate.
- Slip in the unexpected.
- Believe in your pupils and trust them.

CHAPTER 8

Plan the Plan and Abandon the Plan

In my first five years of teaching, before we left to work overseas, I never planned a lesson. Schools just did not expect it. 'Planning books' were called 'record books' and were completed retrospectively, and given in retrospectively in primary schools, on Friday afternoons, and then the head signed and dated them. I always believed our head did not actually read them, and one week I slipped the following into the middle of my plan: 'I can see an elephant sitting in the middle of the playing field.'

My book was returned to me, signed and dated as usual, and with no comment.

In secondary, no one showed the least interest in whether you had a plan or not, as long as the students were doing something if anyone looked in. How much better my offering might have been had I planned from the start. Part of my trouble was that I had specialised in pottery at college and my two-dimensional art had barely moved forward since I left school. I could have taken more interest in what Gordon was doing in the adjoining art room, but the culture of the school discouraged fraternising. He never visited me, and I never visited him, although when we bumped into each other in the storeroom it was always a perfectly friendly experience.

I never knew if anyone of those 50 staff ever wrote a lesson plan.

I do recommend planning – certainly in your head and certainly prior to entering the classroom (unlike practice in the 1960s when we sat on our desks at the front of the room and 'chatted' with the class until inspiration came).

The more you plan, the better the lesson proceeds on the whole. I do not mean more 'objectives' and more detail of the main activity; if you know your stuff the activity might be a brief reference. I only plan in more detail when I am unsure of the content or think I may have forgotten a detail. What I do mean is that a teacher should plan a sequence of linked shifts in direction to span the whole lesson from opening until plenary time. The more changes in direction, the better you will hold the class's attention. There are, of course, exceptions to this advice such as when the class are producing an extended piece of work to be finished in one session.

The first 'must' to address is the massive confusion with regard to the term 'objectives'. The introduction of 'objectives' to lesson planning was ill-thought through and poorly introduced. There is only one objective for a lesson and that is how you intend the pupils to be 'different' at the end of the lesson. What is the new skill or knowledge you are introducing – or consolidating. Whatever that is, it is both the objective of the lesson and the focus of the plenary.

A safe way to ensure the clarity of this is to open the lesson by saying something like:

'In the plenary of this lesson, I shall ask you to explain how to...' *or*

'At the end of this lesson, I shall expect you to be able to prove to a friend that you now know about...' *or*

'At the end of this lesson, I will expect everyone to give me a detailed report with illustrations to explain how...'

And then be sure to leave time for the plenary to take place *and* to ensure that whatever the pupils are asked to *do* in the body of the lesson is a step towards that learning. I have observed many a lesson where the review in the plenary had nothing to do with the initially stated objective. In addition, I have never understood the time-worn WALT and WILF of lesson planning. 'We are learning today' and 'what I am looking for'. Why would I be looking for anything other than what we are learning today? This sort of muddled thinking renders the objective of no use to the pupils. Which do they focus on? What is the priority?

An effective two-day history/English lesson activity might, therefore, look as follows:

1. In the plenary, I shall be expecting you to be able to give a three-minute talk about Florence Nightingale.

2. I tell the story briefly or we all read the story together.

3. We watch a short YouTube video about her.

4. Pupils discuss and identify key points about the work of Florence Nightingale.

5. Pupils copy three (or four – you should base the number required on your knowledge of your class) different but relevant drawings, and write beneath each what it relates to in the story or they match statements to their drawings by number system e.g. any three or four of the following: 'Florence Nightingale at night with the lamp'; 'Florence Nightingale writing a letter by a soldier's bed'; 'A nurse washing her hands thoroughly'; 'A row of beds with soldiers in, very close together'; 'The front of a nurses' training college'.

6. Pupils draft their speech (one good paragraph).

7. Pupils read their draft to each other and comment.

8. Pupils re-draft neatly and accurately.

9. Pupils read their paragraph at least three times.

10. Teacher shows how to build a mnemonic to help them to remember the points they wish to cover e.g. lamp / letters / cleanliness / crowded / training = LLCCT.

11. Three pupils present to class on a voluntary basis in the plenary.

12. At the start of the next session, three more present. At the close, three more present.

13. Objective for next session: 'At the end of this session, I expect you to present a detailed passage with illustration on the work of Florence Nightingale'.

14. Review the previous learning, using LLCCT.

15. Watch a new video clip; review.

16. Pupils revisit their speech, using LLCCT.

17. Pupils write unsupported. Illustrate as appropriate.

18. Pupils exchange writing; read their partner's and comment.

19. Pupils proof and edit their own work.
20. Plenary: objective is restated, and the work is given in.
21. Three more pupils present their speeches.

Similarly, an effective two-day geography/English lesson activity might, therefore, look as follows:

1. In the plenary, I will expect you to show us all an A3 poster illustrating the living coral reef, explaining how it is being damaged and how people could better protect it.

2. Research the coral reef on the internet: what is it made of? Where is it usually located in an ocean? Why is it in shallow water?

3. Identify and illustrate four (six?) different types of coral and note what colour they are.

4. Identify and illustrate three (five?) fish that live on the reef.

5. Identify and illustrate three other living creatures found on the reef.

6. Plan your poster carefully, transferring all the results of your research onto it. Will illustrations and notes be in boxes? In cloud shapes? In random shapes?

7. Show it to your learning partner and talk through what you found.

8. Use colour on your illustrations.

9. Give the poster a title.

10. Use pen to write names under the illustrations and any facts you discovered.

11. Make a line round three walls of the classroom, holding up your posters, and I will choose two people to talk through what they chose to put on their posters.

12. The next session: in the plenary, I will expect you to present an encyclopaedic report on the Great Barrier Reef. You will need to find out:
    • Where it is located.
    • Why it is exceptional.
    • How long it is.
    • How it is getting damaged.
    • What people could do to protect it better.

13. Beneath your report present an illustration of a section of living reef.

14. I will ask three children to read out their reports and then all books will be given in for me to read.

Review and evaluate your teaching against the pupils' progress and depth of knowledge in the objective/s given for the two plenaries.

Standards

The important point about teaching in this semi-integrated way is that you must have high expectations. Every piece of work should be the best the child can produce. Handwriting should be as neat and accurate as the child can do. Illustrations should be carefully drawn, neat and as accurate as the child is capable of. Labels should be clear and neat. If lines are used, for example to box in text or to label a diagram, a ruler should be used.

These high expectations are crucial from the first days that you take over a new class. Run a handwriting activity in the second week after taking over a new class.

Handwriting Activity

1. On Monday morning, put a four- or six-line verse on the whiteboard (preferably a funny one – limericks can be good).

2. Ask the class to copy it down (in ink from Year 3 up) on lined paper and put their names on.

3. Blu Tack all along the bottom of the windows or in 'dead' space below display boards.

4. All walk along and examine everyone's handwriting, showing good manners and respect.

5. After lunch, teach an important point that relates to the most common handwriting error.

6. Ask the class to re-copy the verse, improving their handwriting.

7. Blu Tack the new verse beneath their first effort and compare the two. Did they improve?

8. Walk along the row, comparing everyone's first and second piece.
9. The next morning, teach a second point or repeat the first if necessary.
10. Ask the class to re-copy the verse, improving their handwriting again.
11. Take down the second version and Blu Tack the third below the first.
12. Compare their own first and third versions and then do the same for the rest of the class.
13. After lunch, teach a new point that many are not getting correct.
14. Ask the children to write the verse again for the fourth time, improving their handwriting.
15. Repeat from 7 to 12.
16. Repeat twice on days three, four and five.
17. Compare the tenth version with the first version, is there a dramatic improvement?
18. Use what you have noted to plan a series of handwriting lessons.
19. Repeat the activity termly or half termly as necessary.
20. Keep each child's final 'best' handwriting as a benchmark when reading children's work across the curriculum and to show to a child if the quality of their handwriting is slipping.

Integrated Days

A semi-integrated approach to teaching may now be planned.

By dedicating one week a month (or three days, or however much time you are able) to an integrated study that encompasses, for example, geography, history, English opportunities, maths opportunities and science, you can set up a 'mini-menu' of expectations and give the class one or two sessions a day when they can tackle the 'project' in any sequence they wish, spending as much or as little time each day on different aspects as long as, by the final day, all is finished to a high standard.

An example of this might be:

The Aztecs

Geography

1. Where did they live? Identify the main country/countries on maps of the world.
2. Trace a map of the world, labelling the seven continents and five main oceans.
3. Draw a new map of Mexico and South America.
4. Colour the areas where the Aztecs lived.
5. Label three or more sites of ancient Aztec ruins.

History

1. Who were the Aztecs?
2. Draw and label a picture of an Aztec in their finery.
3. Who were their enemies?
4. How were their pyramids different from Egyptian pyramids?
5. Write about three aspects of Aztec life.

English

1. Imagine you go on a holiday to Mexico.
2. On a walk through the jungle to find the Aztec ruins, you and your friend stumble across an unknown group of Aztecs still living in some ruins.
3. Write your adventure.
4. Write an encyclopaedic report on Aztec pyramids.

Maths

1. Study what we know about the Aztec use of measures in farming.

2. Use non-standard measures to measure things in the classroom, the hall and the playground (spans and strides).

3. Measure your span and your stride in standard measures and calculate roughly how long the distances would be in standard measures.

Science

1. Study examples of each of the flora and fauna of Mexico, producing labelled drawings and notes.

2. Study the climate of Mexico and compare temperatures with those in England and those in Antarctica.

When this plan is complete, you must identify which parts the class should already know, which they could research themselves and which will need teaching before they can successfully complete the task. You can also identify which parts you need to do more research on.

Use one other session a day to teach the required aspects and to review any that they may have forgotten.

Children love having the ability to take some control of their learning and to make choices. Tell them the only thing they are not allowed to do is nothing, and that if they work hard, they will do something very exciting on Friday afternoon. You then give them three choices on Friday afternoon, for example to use modelling media to make decorated Aztec pots, to use blocks of clay or Lego to build an Aztec pyramid or to make a paper collage of a wealthy Aztec in their finery, including gold, silver and other fine papers in the choices. This is what I would describe as a 'mini-menu system' or a mini challenge.

Flexible Activities to Fill the Gaps in any Lessons in any Subjects

Even before you start your first placement, make sure you have a bank of quick-fire independent activities that can be used as time fillers or as buffers between any two lengthy academic activities. Obviously, art-related activities work well but be aware that constant use of one subject may devalue that subject. Some of my favourites are:

1. Centre Patterns

Children start with a circle in the centre of the paper and build out in complete circular rings of each shape they choose, for example various petal shapes, triangular shapes or diamond shapes. Some may be larger than others and have a circle or small square inside. Keep going until the pattern reaches and overspills the edge. Then start back at the centre and colour outwards in one colour per whole row using pencil crayons, wax crayons or thin felt tips. It can be especially effective to limit the range of colours they use, by giving a choice e.g. oranges, yellows and browns; purples and blues; reds, oranges and yellows or blues and greens. The additional benefit of these is that they can be started and stopped at any time, so that they may only be used for a five- or ten-minute slot and then brought out again the next time they are needed. I recommend you collect them and save them (names on the back) as they may get 'lost' or damaged in the children's trays.

2. Times Tables

Teach them at first (2x, 10x, 5x, 11x, 3x, 4x, 6x, 7x, 8x, 9x, 12x). As soon as they know three tables, start 'beat myself quizzes'. Fire mixed up tables questions at them and they write the answers. Then you ask the questions again and they shout the answers and mark their own in a different colour or type of writing tool. The next time, use the same questions but in a different order and the third time in a new order again. See if they score more each time, then change the questions. Up to six for Year 1, eight to ten for Year 2 and ten to twelve for everyone else.

3. Sketching

Have flowers, plants or leaf arrangements in your classroom. Use these as a focus for sketching. Or put a picture of a tree with no leaves large on the whiteboard (Google: 'drawings of trees') or an animal or bird. Sketching should always be in pencil and all should have rubbers.

4. How Many Words of Three Letters or More Can You Make...

Give a long word on the whiteboard and children list all the words, of three letters or more, that they can make using only letters that are in the word and each letter only the same number of times as it occurs in the word. It can be a good idea for them to copy the word onto small whiteboards or scrap paper and put a tick under each letter when used. Of course, the ticks are then rubbed or crossed out so that all letters are available again for the next word. Stress that there should be no adding of 's' to make a plural and no proper names.

It is a good idea to use either an ambitious word they are learning that week or a long word they have met in their other subjects. Make sure they all know what the long word means first. I would use words like 'continually', 'anxiously' and 'geography' in Key Stage 1 and words like 'aggressively', 'sensationally' and 'omnivorous' in Key Stage 2. Children should check words they are not sure about the meaning of in the dictionary. Then go round the class and ask each child for a word. List them on the board and children tick them if they have them, using a different colour or type of writing tool.

Amphibious
ham has mash map mop bop bus bum bush bash pub hub his sip hip sham shop ship spam mob hob sob aim ash soup pious bias him mush hump bump

5. Fastest Finger First Dictionaries

Call out a word and the class race to see who can find it in the dictionary first. They shoot a hand up and you ask them to read the definition. Then fire another word at them. Choose words you think most won't know but that are relevant for them. Remember to check they are in the younger dictionaries, some in Key Stage 1 have a limited range.

There are many other activities like these, I recommend you make a bank of them and keep them handy at all times.

My Top Tips for Planning

- Always plan at least one more activity than you think time allows, you can always use it the next day but there is nothing worse than a lesson finishing early and you having nothing 'up your sleeve'.

- Don't write more than you need to teach the lesson and to respond to the children's understanding and ideas.

- Always make sure you know more about the subject than you expect the children to learn so that you can be responsive to questions or comments.

- Always be prepared to respond to the children's interest in the subject, to go 'off plan' if it is appropriate and do not 'fob them off' and say, 'No, we are learning about this.'

- Always have short time fillers available if needed.

- Consider trying short integrated periods when the time is right.

CHAPTER 9

Differentiation

It has always been my feeling that far too much fuss is made about differentiation, and that it is not as difficult as it is made out to be. There are usually three options for the differentiation of any task:

1. Differentiation by Task

This approach involves planning modified forms of the expected task for the less able child or children. The questions to ask yourself are: is that child still getting the same experiences and opportunities as the rest of the class? Might they be suffering as a result of the teacher's low expectation? Is their task purely a holding activity to give you and the rest of the class space?

2. Differentiation by Support

This approach involves planning the same activity for the whole class while providing active support for the less able child or children. This might be a teaching assistant or learning support assistant, if you are fortunate enough to have a second adult in your classroom. Of course, you will need time to fully brief this person on how they might best support the child or group, and what your expectation is for the children to apply some independent learning and decision making.

If you were going to rely on providing the support yourself, don't! This is not effective or efficient. There will be other distractions, other pupils may need quick answers or explanations, a few children may take advantage of your preoccupation with the support group and so on. Do what you should be doing – managing a calm and industrious workspace and responding to pupil need.

The most effective form of support in most classrooms is peer support, and my preferred approach is allowing the class to make their choices of whom they work with. You will need to be clear in your own mind as to how much support pupils may give each other, how you will know what contribution each pupil made – if you need to know that – and whether some parts of the activity should still be completed individually. For example, the pairs may discuss and plan together but then work separately on their own solution. They could be allowed to interact freely as they work, or they could be given set points in the work where they stop and discuss their progress, sharing their work so far with each other.

This form of differentiation protects a pupil's self-esteem as the whole class will be talking quietly, so they are not being singled out. It also allows you to interact with the small number of pupils who would benefit from that – making suggestions and checking understanding – because all the class are busy exploring their knowledge and ideas.

In addition, the more able child strengthens their own understanding through supporting the less able so both pupils benefit.

3. Differentiation by Outcome

This is the approach to differentiation that often gets the most criticism, but I am rather a fan of it. If you know all your class really well, including their pace when working hard, their capability at problem solving, research, presentation, illustration and any other features of the lesson plan you have devised, then you should know who may struggle to complete the allocated tasks within the time available. A discreet word with class members who may need it will then clarify for them whether a) you are providing the introductory paragraph and they should proceed from there or b) they should start at the beginning but may not need to work on the closing part of the activities or c) they do not need to provide the section that focuses on the historical aspect of the subject, or the mathematical aspect or the scientific aspect – varying the part that is not essential from focus to focus. Very often you may, in fact, find that these pupils will manage to complete all parts of the task (although some may be in less detail) as the pressure has been taken from them.

This form of differentiation also protects the pupil's self-esteem as they are seemingly doing the same work as everyone else, so there is no stigma.

Most teachers will use a combination of models two and three during the school week. The important point is to monitor a) the child's individual response to the work and how much they have to rely on their peers for support and b) the child's response and achievement when allocated the different approaches to work to see if one or another gleans a better response and a higher standard of work.

Differentiation for the Gifted Child

Very few classes contain a gifted child, in fact most schools may only have one, or at the most two, gifted children at one point in time. Nevertheless, they may have a significant number of high ability children whose needs may be under-catered for if planning and activities are always matched to the ability of the majority of the class.

In *Chapter 13 – Marking and Assessment* I tell the story of Stuart – whom I believed to be a gifted child. I rationalised that my misconception that Stuart was gifted came because I did not have a true picture in my head of what more privileged eleven year olds were capable of achieving. In this context of differentiation for needs, however, Stuart still did need work differentiated for his ability to stretch and challenge him, purely because he was far above the ability of the majority of his Year 6 class. So, the issue here is not so much 'Is a child gifted or not?' as 'Is this child capable of being stretched and challenged further than the work pitched for the majority of the class?'

Higher ability pupils should be given additional challenge in the content and quality of what they actually produce, rather than just always being expected to write more. The solution of asking them to write an additional paragraph about the feeding habits of the lesser spotted something or other is not differentiation, it is buying 'holding time' so that the able child does not finish too early. If, however, the additional challenge requires further and more challenging research or if it requires inference and conclusions to be drawn, this would provide the additional challenge required to stretch the child. For example, the additional paragraph might have its own specification that requires thorough research into the feeding habits and food sources in the wild, plus an analysis of the current impact of climate change on the lesser spotted whatever, with a predictive summary of the risk of extinction and steps that people could be taking currently to avoid this.

The risk for the classroom teacher is that high ability pupils may get bored with the daily basic diet of the class – and the gifted pupil certainly will. Fortunately, a truly gifted child will probably have been adapting their view on life, and the activities on offer, both at home and at school for most of the years they have lived. Most will continue to do so in your class, so that their work is rarely the same as the majority, but stands out. For some, however, they will hurry through the mundane tasks set and then bury themselves in a book – which we will allow because we recognise that they are 'a fast worker'. The worst scenario is the gifted but extremely bored or unhappy boy, who may often under perform in the work set but excel in disrupting the class, frequently, quietly and very cleverly. Justin may have been an example of this pupil in *Chapter 11 – Managing Behaviour.*

My advice would be to tell the gifted pupil you expect more from them from the start, discreetly acknowledging their high ability, and plan to challenge them from the start with firm bottom lines regarding completion and standards. Do not assume that because a pupil is highly able, they will necessarily want to become the 'teaching assistant' to support the less able. In fact, they could be exactly the wrong person for that role. I write as someone with a gifted eldest sister who was intensely irritated by all lesser beings, and totally uninterested in making her highly sophisticated scientific and mathematical knowledge accessible to anyone else. And remember – gifted does not always mean well presented. The handwriting of most doctors is illegible – as is my sister's.

Home Learning During Lockdown for Covid-19

During the lockdown we experienced during the pandemic, my daughter and son-in-law taught their two children throughout the mornings, using materials supplied by the school. I taught them in the foundation subjects in the afternoons, which allowed their parents to complete work calls and other business matters.

Towards the end of the first lockdown we had one of our best two days. My seven-year-old grandson unexpectedly missed all Monday afternoon when I had planned to introduce the new theme of Antarctica – I was trying to choose studies the children are less likely to do in school. I changed my plan at the last minute and asked his older sister, aged ten, to research and plan a lesson that she would teach him about Antarctica the next day. She loved it and made a very good PowerPoint for her lesson with two YouTube videos seeded in and lots of facts. The next day, they both loved her teaching him and it gave rise to excellent discussions, including the Earth's orbit round the Sun, and why it never gets dark in the middle of summer and never gets light in the middle of winter, using the globe to illustrate the points.

Teaching Children with English as an Additional Language (EAL)

I have had a long self-debate as to whether this section should be in 'planning' or in 'differentiation'. Of course, as they are both integral to each other – as the best differentiation is well planned – perhaps it should be in both.

It is crucial to note that children learning in English as an additional language are of all abilities. There will be very high achievers and the rare gifted child. There will also be children of average ability and a small number who are really struggling to learn for one reason or another. However, when the children are new to English (usually because they have just arrived in England), they are all in the same situation – unable to demonstrate their abilities in English a) because they can't understand what you are talking about and b) because they cannot communicate anything they already know back to you.

Many of us do what I did at first, in my ignorance – 'ignore' the new arrival (apart from a warm smile here or there) until they begin to understand and speak in English! This is clearly wrong and there is a lot you can do to help the child to make quicker progress and to achieve some success in the early stages. This is a very difficult time for all pupils in this situation, and will be stressful for some. In schools with a high percentage of pupils with English as an additional language, systems will usually be in place to support any newly arriving children or the child still in the early stages of learning English, so the best thing to do is to check with your mentor or a senior leader to establish what the usual provision is.

The following are all elements of best practice in this situation:

- Sit the new child with another child who speaks the same language (if possible) and encourage them to talk quietly in their first language after each input from you. Do not be afraid that they will be 'off-task'. Just as you can tell if the group at the back of the room are 'on-task' or 'off-task' even though you cannot hear what is being said, you will be able to tell with this pairing too.
- Identify a teaching assistant who speaks the child's first (home) language or, failing that, a parent. With the help of leadership, prepare a list of questions they might ask the child to establish how well educated the child is in their first language, their experiences, preferences, and achievements in their previous schooling.
- When planning lessons, ask yourself what you can do to help the new to English pupil to understand what is going on. Can you use pictures? Can you mime something? Can you ask some of the class to mime? Is there an appropriate video? Can you get key word translations from the internet, a bilingual member of staff or a local resident? Key words are the crucial words of the learning. See the example below. Be very careful if trying to translate phrases or sentences as meanings can change in different circumstances. If I were to teach about giraffes, however, I would certainly want the word 'giraffe' in Chinese, Arabic and any other language that was represented in my class, and possibly the words 'neck' and 'leaves'. Using a combination of all the above is clearly the most effective solution. You might then mime a giraffe stretching up and eating. You will be surprised how quickly use of these strategies will become second nature and also, how much they will improve access for many other children in the class.
- Find out if the child knows what a giraffe is in their home language and use the term in conjunction with the English when you are teaching.

- Be aware that, although a child may seem to be quite proficient in English, they may only be using it in school. It is called 'surface competency' when a child has the superficial language of daily classroom use but does not have a deeper understanding. Thus, the child may be able to understand and reply appropriately to routine daily questions but have no experience of the technical language and names of the jungle or the rainforest or of sailing ships and voyages of the past and so on. This is where thoughtful planning with supplementary materials or strategies can really help.

Example of a Two-Lesson Plan of Support for Pupils with EAL

The Amazon Rainforest – Exemplar Lesson One

Introduction

Map of the world – pupils (with help as appropriate) identify and name out loud as a class:

- The United Kingdom/British Isles.
- The home countries of all class members not born in England.
- Name/identify five major oceans and seven continents.
- Name/identify lines of latitude, if already introduced.
- Name/identify Canada, USA, Mexico.
- Name/identify Brazil.
- Repeat if needed and tell class they will need to know all the names in the plenary.

Body

- Teacher traces round South America with finger, all to name.
- Teacher draws South America on whiteboard or flip chart.
- Pupils draw South America on A4 paper.
- Teacher draws round area covered by rainforest and demonstrates shading in green and labels.
- Pupils shade in area of rainforest and label.

- Teacher shows a picture of Francisco de Orellana's ship and a picture of him.
- Class draw in the River Amazon on the map, teacher says 'longest river' stretching arms and then pointing round the world on a globe.
- Class say 'longest river'.
- Teacher explains in simple words and by pointing that de Orellana was the first man from Europe to explore the River Amazon and gives the date.
- Pupils copy the picture.

Plenary
- Teacher points to all countries, continents and oceans named in the introduction and pupils name.
- Teacher points round the Amazon Rainforest and pupils name.
- Teacher asks what is special about the River Amazon and pupils demonstrate with arms, saying 'Longest river in the world.'

The Amazon Rainforest – Exemplar Lesson Two

Introduction
- Teacher shows a map of the Amazon Rainforest and explains that by the end of the lesson the class should be able to describe the climate and to name at least four (or six) animals that live in the rainforest and recognise them when they see pictures.

Body
- Teacher explains in words with key words and signs (Google: rainforest, six, animals) that the children are to use the internet to research the animals and write a short encyclopaedia report on each (one paragraph only on habitat, diet and habits).
- Class work in pairs to complete research, with each of the pair producing their fact sheet, labelling and colouring their drawings. The new to English child is supported by a bilingual adult or child if possible

and if not, works with a co-operative, more able child who will at least enable them to complete the research, drawing and labelling, and help them to repeat the names of six animals in English several times until confident.

- Teacher names the animals both in English and in the child's first language (translations through search engine). Establish if child knows the animal in first language already through pointing at the child and the pictures.
- Teacher explains that the children are to research the climate of the rainforest and compare it with England. Teacher takes facts and records on the whiteboard or flip chart. Children then research English climate and teacher records the facts.
- Work in pairs and then class discussion to compare the climates.

Plenary
- Teacher shows illustrations of a range of animals of the rainforest on the whiteboard.
- Class name as many as they can between them, all together, then teacher moves round the whiteboard at random, asking children to name the animals in turn round the room.
- All name once more saying name in English and then in the child's first language (written phonetically on the board).
- If time, confident children give some facts about an animal of their choice.
- Teacher collects the fact sheets in for marking.

Be aware that you will make small mistakes in your efforts to be inclusive; try not to brood on them but rather to learn from them. When I was teaching in the Bradford middle school, I received a new pupil from China in my class. He did not speak a word of English, and no one in the school spoke Chinese, but, luckily, he brought me an envelope with his name on in phonetic English, with his lunch money inside. I was so welcoming and inclusive with that boy, forever saying things like:

'Let me come and help you to do that, Keean Wancan.'

'Come and let me show you this, Keean Wancan.'

It was only when his mother came in to see me that I discovered I had spent half a term calling this poor, bewildered boy 'Dinner Money'!

My Top Tips for Differentiation

- Try different methods with a child to see which appear to work best for them.
- Try not to rely on yourself for support to a child for more than a few minutes.
- Do not just give extra work to the most able child but rather plan in additional challenge.
- Always ask yourself if any work set is just a 'holding' activity.
- Plan access to the learning for the child who does not yet fully understand English, mainly through seating with another speaker of the same first language, through key word translation and through use of pictures and mime.
- Use translation sites on the internet to find key words.

CHAPTER 10

Classroom Organisation

Seating

How you physically organise your classroom and class seating is almost always a matter of personal choice, but when you first start teaching how do you make such a choice? As you walk round the school, keep an eye on other classrooms. Are they all arranged the same way? It is also a good time to check out displays – more about that later.

In almost all primary schools, tables or desks are arranged in blocks of six seats round three tables. The secret is always to have the third table across the far ends of the first two tables – at the end furthest away from the point where you mainly teach – which is usually slightly to one side of the whiteboard. Then the 'open' end, where there are no chairs and no children sit, is pointing towards you and the whiteboard and no one will have their back to the you or the whiteboard. Angle your blocks of tables so that all the seats are facing the whiteboard, two up the outside edges of the tables pointing forwards, and two across the table that is across the furthest end.

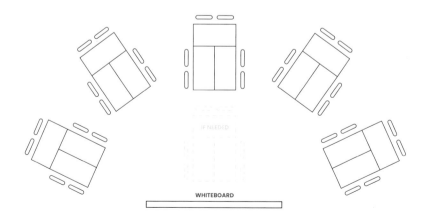

IF NEEDED

WHITEBOARD

If the classroom is large enough, it is really helpful to arrange the five or six blocks of tables in a fan-shaped semi-circle, all slightly angled towards the front. This leaves a clear space in the centre for presentations and performances, and for children to gather and sit on the floor for more intimate input. If the room is not large enough for that, one block of tables will need to be in the centre space.

I prefer to let the children sit in friendship groups, in other words where they want. Many teachers, however, have seating plans and make seating decisions based on ability groupings or on peer support or on behaviour management. I think the decision is best made by the teacher involved. Once seating is determined, however, I do try not to keep moving children around. As a species, humans like security and a feeling of their own space and base. I think it is unsettling and can be hurtful to keep moving children unless there is a good reason.

Behaviour management is a good reason! If two children are becoming particularly disruptive, and the quiet word technique plus the praising of other pupils' good behaviour has failed to make a difference, then I discreetly warn the children that I am going to split them up if they can't manage their behaviour. You need to have enough seating in your classroom to be able to do this effectively. It is not fair for a perfectly well-behaved child to be moved from their chosen seat so that you can re-seat a disruptive child. When setting up your classroom at the start, try to have two spare seats and encourage children to leave one empty on two different blocks of tables near the front of the classroom to allow for flexible moves.

Initially, you may only need to move one of the two disruptive pupils, and you might only move them for one day or a few days or one week in the first instance, before letting them return to their chosen seat and seeing if they can now manage their behaviour better. If necessary, however, make the move more permanent. It is more effective to move the child who is actually sitting between their friend and the others on the table, causing slight isolation for the one who remains on the original block.

The key to success is to watch the pair carefully for a while before making the move. Is one more the instigator than the other? Who starts the trouble? It is definitely more helpful to move the more disruptive child, providing you have a space on a table of sensible children who are likely to ignore them. If you leave the disruptor, they are very likely to turn their attentions to the other children on the table. If it can be arranged, it is also useful to have more disruptive children on the outside edge of the two tables nearest the whiteboard, where they know you can see them clearly at all times and you can see what they are doing – whether they have something under the table and so on. For more on behaviour management see *Chapter 11 – Managing Behaviour.*

Keep the classroom tidy. Clear out cupboards once a term, and ensure there is space to put everything away. If something has not been used for a year, why are you keeping it? Bring in pot plants and an occasional bunch of flowers to make the tops and windowsills as attractive as possible. Interesting natural objects, or retro objects from a car boot sale, can also contribute to the 'homely' feel, and give a new dimension for a quick sketch or for a longer observational drawing session. A globe is also attractive and useful.

Moving Furniture

Children in Key Stage 2 should learn to move the furniture around quickly and efficiently without too much fuss or noise. In Key Stage 1, you will need to do the job while the children are not in the room, so it is all the more important to have sufficient floor space left near the front for the class to relocate onto the floor for some input, discussions and story time without having to rearrange furniture.

For meaningful discussions in Key Stage 2, I am a huge fan of re-organising seating into an open horseshoe round three sides of the room with the opening at the front of the room. In most classes, it may need to be a double horseshoe to fit everyone in. It is not difficult to move the tables and chairs from six-seater blocks into an open horseshoe, although it may be a little chaotic at first. I would, therefore, plan the move carefully in my head in the first instance, and manage the whole operation, table by table, the first time.

Move the blocks at the back of the classroom first, so that they become a line of three tables joining another line of three tables. This will ensure that there is sufficient space. There is nothing worse than building from the sides and finding you can't fit the last one or two tables in the middle at the back. If the side rows are coming too far forward, create an inner horseshoe or one large block in the centre space. Try not to make this too close to the back horseshoe as that discourages interaction from children in the rear.

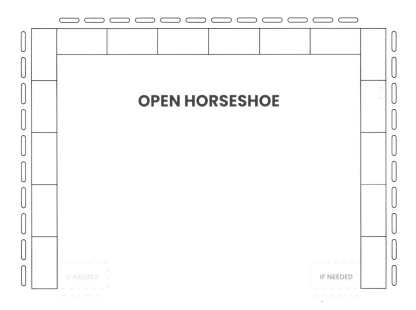

Children need to be taught the skills of discussion and debate – more on that in *Chapter 12 – Discussion and Debate*.

For informal discussions, peer discussion and small group discussion there is no need to move furniture. For drama and role play, or for more sensitive inputs such as in personal, social and health education or religious education, the tables need to go right back to the walls with the chairs on the inside of the space in a circle. Some tables may need to go on top of others, depending on the size of the room. If that is the case, make sure the top ones are turned upside down (table top to table top) so that they are much less likely to be dislodged. To create more space, place the chairs – again upside down – on top of the tables and use the floor for circular seating while you explain to the class what it is you wish them to do.

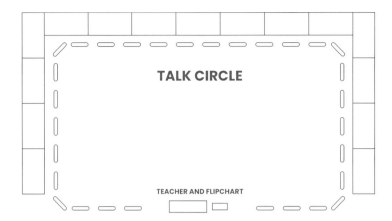

TALK CIRCLE

TEACHER AND FLIPCHART

Displays

Display is a highly important part of the classroom environment. Remember you and the children spend more waking time in your classroom on a school day than you do in your sitting room at home. The classroom needs as much attention to making it an attractive environment as your sitting room does.

As you move around the school, keep an eye on the displays on the corridor and in the classrooms. Do not be afraid to ask members of staff if you may have a closer look at their displays if any look particularly interesting or attractive to you. The issue of display will have been addressed in training for most of you, and it is always a surprise to me when a young teacher has not had that input. Do ask your mentor for advice. Seek out whoever does the corridor displays – they are usually of very high quality and that person may be willing to advise, and even support, in the early days.

Most schools have one or even two 'teacher INSET' days before the new school year starts, and staff are almost always given at least half a day to get their classrooms prepared. However, if I were starting a new position, I would always ask if I could go in to school one or two days prior to the official start. Most headteachers will be in before the start of term, and are happy for staff to be in preparing their rooms for the new term.
One of the first jobs you should do is to cover your display boards with backing paper.

The most important part of a display is the children's work and backing paper should not detract from that. My preference is plain black paper on all boards and failing that a dark blue or beige. I do not feel that reds and yellows complement all pupils' work and certainly not work with colour. Some teachers designate boards to subjects and put titles on them to indicate this. I like to be more flexible as that practice dictates how many pieces of work you are able to display. If a class has worked particularly hard on an aspect of learning, I prefer to display everyone's work. Of course, at the start of the school year you have no work to display and thus you will either leave the boards empty or you will use commercial displays such as key words and ambitious vocabulary for English, times tables and key words for maths and relevant illustrations and key words for the other initial teaching you will be doing.

It is extremely important that children's work is displayed – and displayed well. Every classroom should have access to a guillotine, and in the case of artwork it can be a good idea to trim a small amount from round the edge of the child's work, particularly of paintings. This enables an A4 piece of work to fit onto an A4 mount and the same with A3, as the piece of work is now slightly smaller than the standard size. If the school can afford it, a double mount is very effective, with a narrow black border round the piece of work and then a slightly wider white border. This, of course, means you have used three sheets of paper for every one item on display and these days schools may not afford that. A solution can be a single white mount but rule a black felt-tip border close to the edges of the piece of work. If you use good quality paper and if you do not glue the backing on but rather pin the work and the backing paper onto the wall together, you can usually recycle the backing paper two or three times. Thus, an A3 piece of white used to back artwork could be trimmed down and become a backing for a piece of A4 writing later that term.

The title on the display board would then be matched to whatever the focus of the work was, for example 'Our Reports on the Amazon Rainforest' or 'If I Ruled the World'. Titles might be made of cut-out letters stencilled round wooden or plastic letters, or you might choose to buy sets of silver letters from art shops or supermarkets.

A good display may be left up for some weeks, so it is not a waste to invest time in this. I would try to change one display at least every half term, but I would not attempt to replace like with like. You will soon recognise when a piece of work the children are producing is of good enough quality to merit being displayed. If you are always expecting 'best' work with a high standard of presentation, illustration and handwriting, you may find you need to change displays more often.

Always put the child's name neatly in one corner of the mount or just below on the backing paper.

Teach your class to take an interest in displays and to treat them with respect and ensure that every child has something on display somewhere at all times.

My Top Tips for Classroom Organisation

- Give every child a dedicated seat or let them choose their own and don't move them unless there are concerns about behaviour.
- Ensure all children can see the whiteboard at all times, without having to turn round.
- Make the classroom environment a pleasant and attractive place to be.
- Keep cupboard tops clean and tidy.
- Invest time and patience in learning to make displays of the highest quality possible.

CHAPTER 11

Managing Behaviour

This chapter on managing pupils' behaviour should be read in conjunction with *Chapter 5 – Fake it to Make It* and *Chapter 10 – Classroom Organisation*. The impression you give to your class and around school is crucial to the image that pupils develop of you. The majority of us were very nervous, or even scared, when we first took responsibility for a class as a 'real' teacher, but the last thing we should do is let the children see that. From day one in a new school we should exude confidence and authority, even though we may not really feel it. If necessary, practise the walk, straight backed, chin held high, making eye contact, a slight smile when appropriate, greeting when appropriate… it may be fake at first, but it becomes a reality very quickly.

The image of a teacher is not – and should not be – the same as the image many of us portrayed as students. We may have sought to be 'cool' and 'with it' when in university, and many of us dressed 'down' or very casually during term time. This is not how we should seek to portray ourselves as teachers if we wish to exude professional competence and confidence. Watch staff as they move around school and interact with their pupils and classes. Identify those you admire and whose image works for you as a professional, and do not be afraid to model yourself on one or two until you develop your own style.

Respond to First Testing of the Boundaries

It is very rare for a new class to 'test out' a new teacher on the first day or two of the new academic year. Usually it is a gradual process, with one or, at most, two pupils slowly starting to test the boundaries. The first rule is – make your boundaries clear. The second rule is – do not ignore the first minor incidents. Usually, they will come in the form of whispering while you are talking, talking when you have asked for silence, being slow to respond when asked to do something (like getting books out, putting them away or establishing calm) or deliberately dropping something on the floor, like a book, a pencil or a ruler.

You must respond to these small misdemeanours.

In the first week and for the first instance from a child, it may be little more than a stare and a quiet word. Moving towards the pupil is a good idea: lean forward slightly, make eye contact and say something quietly, like: 'Pick it up.' *or* 'I asked for quiet.' *or* 'I said put your books away please.'

This need not be in an angry or hostile voice, but it should be firm and without a smile. If the child makes a comment back (other than 'Sorry') unless it is very relevant, ignore it, lean a little further and repeat your instruction in the same tone, maintaining eye contact.

Similar behaviour is needed if you suspect one or two pupils are 'off-task' or distracted. Move purposefully around the room – not necessarily straight to their table – and position yourself slightly behind and to one side and stand there. You will now be able to see what the pupils are doing, whether they have anything they should not have out or whether they have, in fact, started work. Often, your position alone will be sufficient to defuse the situation as it is unnerving for a pupil to be unable to see you but to know you are there. If, however, the pupil does not settle to work, move round into the eye line, make eye contact, lean forward slightly, and say something like: 'Is there a good reason why you are not working like everyone else in the class?'

Speak quietly and calmly. Humiliating a potentially disruptive pupil will often challenge them to behave worse or even to attempt conflict with you in the early days. If they do not respond after the second repeat, pick up their book and suggest, politely, that if they move nearer to the front, you will be better able to help them. Take the books to a front, empty seat (pre-arranged in your classroom organisation, see *Chapter 10 – Classroom Organisation*) and stand by the chair, indicating it with your hand. This will very rarely happen in the early days of a new class and if you work hard to win the class over to your 'side' it may never happen.

Class Rules

Within the first three days, it is a good idea to agree class rules. Consulting the class with regard to rules is always good policy, but you need to have clear 'bottom lines' yourself which must be included. If you are teaching in Key Stage 2 or above, most pupils do know how they are expected to behave in school but do not always choose to observe the rules. Do check first whether there are some fundamental school rules that apply to all classes and children before you start adding your own.

My 'bottom lines' were always:
1. Nobody talks while the teacher is talking to the class.
2. Nobody talks while a pupil is presenting an answer in a whole class lesson.
3. Nobody disrespects anyone in the class, whether by comment or behaviour.
4. Keep your space and tray tidy and leave your jackets on the pegs provided.
5. All work is 'best' work unless you are told otherwise. It should be neat, accurate and careful.

The fewer rules you have, the easier it is to enforce them. The 'disrespect' rule is very useful as almost all inappropriate behaviours can come under that rule – the pupil is disrespecting you, their peers, someone's property or someone's 'space'.

If someone is infringing a rule, it is a good idea to move to the displayed rules, point to the one they are infringing and raise an eyebrow. Only speak if that has no effect. It will often be sufficient to say:
'Rule two, Dominic,' again in a managed and measured tone but firmly.

If they are not catching your eye or seem to be ignoring you, say their name firmly and clearly while pointing to the relevant rule.

Be firm about rules, keep them simple and make them work for you. You will need to decide whether to share your bottom lines with the class before asking if anyone has any more suggestions, but that can lead to the development of a long list of rules, and it is inadvisable to ignore any suggestions. The agreeing of rules is an opportunity for your first circle time, pushing the furniture back to the walls and arranging the chairs in one large circle. You should have your chair in the circle too, with a flip chart beside you, and you should record the suggested rules on the flip chart.

Ask the class why we need a few rules for our classroom. Respond positively to every suggestion but push the discussion until you get to a useful statement. For example, you might say something like:
'That's a very important point Lucy, well done. Lucy said,
"_ _ _ _ _ _ _ _ _ _ _ _ _ _ _ _ _ _" everyone. Can anyone add to that?'
Don't worry if someone offers a different suggestion instead, simply say:
'Good James, may we come back to that? I was hoping someone could pick up on Lucy's good point. She said, "_ _".'

To encourage early discussion, you need open body language, a slight smile, eye contact with the speaker and turn or lean slightly towards them. Don't rush children and don't be afraid to lead towards answers if necessary.

When you have a reasonable number of potential rules on the flip chart, I suggest you combine some under one or two simple rules that the children can all learn and remember. You will find that most, if not all, will fit under the five examples given in my 'bottom line'. It is now important to scribe the rules, visibly and neatly, and display them prominently at the front of the classroom, making regular reference to them. When you need to address a situation, it can help to ask:
'Which of our agreed rules does this relate to?' Ensure that all the class know all the rules by heart by the end of the second week, if possible.

Facial expressions are very useful in managing behaviour and may need practice for some of us. Ideally, we want to reach the point where most unwanted behaviours in the classroom can be dealt with by a look. If our usual expression is open with warm eyes and a slight smile, a switch to a colder expression with 'dead' eyes and even a slight frown or raised eyebrows can be very effective. As mentioned previously, a single raised eyebrow is especially impactful, but we are not all able to make one eyebrow rise.

Of course, if you look cross or 'cold' all the time you lose the opportunity to use facial expression in behaviour management.

If the raised eyebrow, the 'cold' demeanour and your relocation behind the child, all with a quiet but firm word, haven't worked, and the move of the main instigator to the front of the class failed, you only have one option left and that is to tell the child you need a word with them outside the classroom. This really is a last resort, and – unless you are fortunate enough to have a classroom assistant in the room to stay with the class – do remember to leave the classroom door wide open and to give the class the 'look' and put your finger on your lips as you leave. They will remain quiet because they are hoping to hear what you say.

Position the child (by your own manoeuvring and a point – not by physical means) with their back to the wall to the side of the open door so that they cannot see the class and so that children in the classroom cannot catch their eye. Stand squarely in front, quite close so that they can see little but you (unless social distancing is required) and start by asking why the child is not following the rules agreed by everyone in the class. Depending on their response, you will need to reshape your answer but it may involve a reminder about unacceptable behaviour and pointing out to the child that the only options that may be left to you – if things don't improve – will be to inform the headteacher and/or the parents. Do not raise your voice and do respond more positively if you feel the child is regretting their behaviour.

Finally, move back into more positive, negotiation mode if the attitude of the child feels appropriate, offering options such as returning to their place and working quietly or joining you at the front and working quietly. In the vast majority of cases, the child will choose to return to their place and work quietly. Find a real reason to praise the child as soon as possible, with your warm expression back in place.

If more extreme behaviour persists, you should consult your mentor, year or phase leader or the headteacher. None of us like doing this, it feels like an admission of our personal failure, but it is crucial that behaviour is 'sorted' as speedily as possible, and one disruptive child can upset the balance in a classroom very easily.

I remember one boy I had in my Year 6 class in Kirklees, two years before I joined the local authority. His name was Justin and he was a known disruptive pupil throughout the school. When Justin was in class, I never saw him do or say anything disruptive and yet all around him there was chaos. Children around him – who would behave impeccably on the rare days he was absent – were perpetually 'off-task', sniggering and being a nuisance. I suspected, in reality, that they were afraid of Justin and were trying to ingratiate themselves with him. Some days were so bad that I found myself wishing I did not have to go to school the next day, but of course I did. And this was me as a mature late-40ish woman who had taught for nearly 30 years. On the rare days that Justin was absent from school, the class were totally different – calm and hard working.

When the class left for high school, I gave a sigh of relief and welcomed my next form with open arms. We had a wonderful year together. Justin lasted five weeks in the comprehensive school before being removed and placed in Nortonthorpe Hall – a school for disruptive boys in Kirklees at that time. In those days, secondary teachers were not as prepared to struggle on with serious behavioural issues as primary school teachers.

Everyone Belongs in the Team

After the first few weeks of the first term, routines should be becoming established and small incidents of poor behaviour should be rarer. Your relationship with your pupils should be growing stronger daily, and it is crucial that, whenever the potentially disruptive child is behaving and working, you acknowledge, praise and reward. By this time, you will have forms of sanction in place which may include incentives, rewards and withdrawal of privileges (see *Chapter 6 – Bribery and Penalties*). This will make management of behaviour so much easier, but do remember – difficult children are almost always living difficult lives, and the stronger and warmer the relationship you build with them, the better for you and the child and the class. However, they will always have the occasional storm because – usually – something difficult has happened at home.

If things have not settled in the first term, don't worry. Every new term is a new start – put the 'bottom lines' in place immediately and deal with even the smallest incidents promptly. Even if you never feel totally happy with that first year (I never felt happy about my class management the year I had Justin), still don't worry. The start of the next academic year will see a new class, new rules, new positive approaches and things will get better and better. Remember: it takes five years…

Finally, and most importantly, build a feeling of 'team' or 'family' in your classroom – a feeling of being a part of something important and of belonging. Make the classroom a 'safe' place where everyone is treated with respect and no one shouts at anyone (including you as the teacher). Ideally, it should also be a happy place. When you meet the children at the classroom door at the start of every morning, greet each child warmly by name and with a smile, occasionally making a comment or asking a question, if appropriate. When you dismiss them at the end of the day, wish them a pleasant evening and tell them you look forward to seeing them the next day. Avoid time off school, unless essential, as the children will be disrupted by having a 'strange' teacher. And at least once a week, spend a little time chatting with the class, perhaps at the start of the week about what they did at the weekend or towards the end of the week about what they hope to do at the weekend.

My Top Tips for Managing Behaviour

- Make your boundaries clear from the start.
- Don't ignore first minor infringements.
- Deal with first slips discreetly but firmly.
- Never humiliate children.
- Agree a short set of class rules and display them clearly at the front of the room.
- Ensure all know and understand the rules.
- Point to the relevant rule if raising an issue.
- Praise good behaviour constantly.
- Praise the more difficult child whenever possible and ensure they feel part of the 'family'.
- Remember, there are often stressful circumstances in a child's life if their behaviour is often poor.
- Build a feeling of belonging to something special – a feeling of 'family'.

CHAPTER 12

—————

Discussion and Debate

In *Chapter 10 – Classroom Organisation*, it was advised that children from Year 3 upwards learn to move furniture quickly and without fuss. Teaching them to carry tables (working in twos) and chairs with legs pointing downwards for safety is a key lesson and it is worth taking time to invest in it.

Knowing when you wish to bring the class together on the carpet in front of you, when to form a 'seated on the floor' or a 'chairs in a circle' within the tables and when to rearrange tables to form open horseshoes for debate are important decisions. My advice would be not to disrupt the smooth running of the week by moving all furniture too frequently, and place great importance on the intention to rearrange the room.

Informal Gathering 'on the Carpet'

This is when a teacher asks the class to 'come and sit on the carpet,' with no specific instruction for order or arrangement. Alternatively, you might ask them to sit on the carpet with their 'talk partner' or 'work partner'. The gathering may take place directly in front of the whiteboard, the teacher's desk or chair, or even in the reading corner if that is the only carpeted area. Older children will be perfectly alright directly on an uncarpeted floor, providing it is clean and dry.

These informal gatherings are most often used for:

1. Direct teaching: when the teacher knows that they want the children to turn in different directions to talk in twos, threes or fours for informal discussion and feedback purposes. For example, the teacher may have told the story of Captain James Cook's discovery of the Australian east coast and asked questions related to the story, or

asked them to discuss what life on the ship would be like for so many sailors, or asked them to imagine what it must have been like when The Endeavour hit The Great Barrier Reef, what the sailors will have thought and how they might have saved themselves and the ship.

2. Discussion in response to a part of a story just read. Teachers will often ask questions such as:

    *   'Why do you think that might have happened?'
    *   'What do you think is going to happen next?'
    *   'What would you have done if you were X?'
    *   'What might you find if you went to Z?'

3. Discussion prior to collecting ideas to make a list on the flip chart for a purpose. For example: class rules, animals we might find in Australia or the qualities of a best friend.

4. Analysing a piece of text for shared reading or to glean information or to improve the standard of the piece.

5. Shared writing to build a piece of text together on the flip chart or whiteboard.

6. Teaching a new item of learning so that children may talk together to understand it or to work out answers to questions.

All the above could be achieved equally well whilst still seated at their blocks of tables, but changing the seating is a good way of providing variety and helping the class to re-focus.

Seated on the Floor or Chairs in a Circle Within the Tables

This is often known as 'circle time' in primary schools and is used for several purposes, including:

*   Personal, social and health education.
*   Religious education of a sensitive nature.
*   Discussion regarding issues in the classroom or school.
*   Presentations by members of the class to their peers.
*   Demonstrations and performances.

Children from Reception to Year 4 will normally sit cross legged on the floor, and Upper Key Stage 2 will more usually sit on chairs, unless the culture of the school has maintained floor seating throughout every year. This also precludes the need for the movement of tables to the extremities of the room so that the chairs can be arranged in a circle inside them. This is a job that can take the teacher (and – if they are lucky – a classroom assistant) the whole of their break time or half their lunch time to achieve, and it is not advisable to involve young children in the process. However, Upper Key Stage 2 are quite well able to achieve this arrangement in little over five minutes, with good management and practice. Remember the 'all legs downwards' rule for safety.

Circular seating ensures that no one's view of the teacher, other speaker or performance is inhibited by having another child in front. It encourages more courteous behaviour in open discussion or during the answering of questions, such as only one person speaking at a time, than informal groupings on the floor do. It also enables the teacher to monitor the attention span of all children and to better know when the class are losing concentration.

Open Horseshoes for Debate

This is the most disruptive seating arrangement to organise and with younger children it is not usually used as it requires the movement of all tables into a new, formal arrangement. The aim is to move all tables or desks into a large open 'horseshoe' or three straight sided U-shape, just far enough from the walls or wall furniture so that the chairs can be slipped behind them for the children to be seated behind the tables facing the middle of the room, and therefore facing each other across the room.

If the room is not large enough for all to fit in one horseshoe, a second, smaller horseshoe is built in the middle or one block of tables is put in the middle or two part sides are put at each side of the open end. This arrangement encourages a much more mature and formal discussion and also allows for the pupils to have paper and pens or small whiteboards for note taking or 'voting' if required.

To introduce formal discussion and debate, it is worth reviewing the class rules and discussing the concept of respect. Explain that the point of debate is to hear different points of view and that all opinions are good and deserve respect, and the aim is to come to an agreed way forward if it is an issue under debate. As this is an activity you will usually do with Years 5 or 6, you could make a link to discursive (discussion) writing, which they should already be familiar with, where two sides of an argument are presented.

Initially, the aim is to encourage pupils to want to contribute. It can be a good idea for every child to have a green card 'hand' with a thumb up, on the top of a lollipop stick that they can hold in front of them if they wish to speak. This should not mean, however, that you won't still indicate to a silent side of the horseshoe, or corner, and say:
'Has anyone seated there got an opinion? Did anyone think Mrs Hannigan was correct when she did that – and why?'

Do not ask children to sit with their hands up for significant periods of time.

Subjects for debate might include:
- Incidents in a story the class are reading.
- A person's behaviour in a story the class are reading.
- An incident in a popular TV programme (an excerpt might be played before the debate).
- An incident in the news at the moment.
- An incident in school recently.
- What the class should do for an upcoming assembly or celebration.
- What the class could do to raise money for a charity.
- Where class members would like to go for their visit to the coast.
- What school rule class members would like to see changed and why.
- World issues such as global warming and conservation.

Topics for debate should always be interesting and informative. They should usually follow pre-learning or pre-discussion that may include the watching of videos; children cannot debate if they do not have the knowledge.

When the class have grown familiar with the process of debate, it is very rewarding to introduce dialogic talk to the occasions. This was the work of Professor Robin Alexander in the early 2000s (In 2004, Robin Alexander published his seminal work *Towards Dialogic Teaching: Rethinking Classroom Talk*). This initiative had a significant impact in the schools and areas that adopted it but – due to the massive upheavals in education at the time – it did not achieve the recognition it deserved.

Dialogic talk consists of teaching children the formal language of debate and how to use it. The most effective way that I have found is to give the children a list of the types of phrases to use to open statements, questions and other contributions. Then to give them time to practise informally in small groups at tables before attempting to move it into a horseshoe discussion. When pupils are both comfortable with open discussion in the horseshoe and with using the language of debate, the two can be 'married' quite quickly and successfully.

A list of dialogic phrases might include openings like:
- 'I agree with X's opinion, but I also think that...'
- 'Taking a different point of view on this issue, I think that...'
- 'Referring back to my earlier point...'
- 'Referring back to X's earlier point...'
- 'An alternative point of view might be...'
- 'I agree with the earlier speakers, however I also think that...'
- 'Building on from that interesting point, I think that...' and so on...

My Top Tips for Discussion and Debate
- Develop a culture of respect and good manners.
- Have clear rules about listening and not talking when someone else is.
- Proactively teach dialogic phrases for opening sentences.
- Give a paddle or a card thumbs-up hand for children to indicate they are ready to contribute.
- Always choose interesting topics related to studies or news.
- Praise and encourage.
- Be patient if someone is fumbling and expect the class to be too.

CHAPTER 13

Marking and Assessment

Every school has its own attitudes and accepted practices for assessment, and a key part of your induction to a new school should be induction into when and how pupils across the whole school are assessed.

Chris Dyson, Headteacher at Parklands Primary School, Seacroft in Leeds, lists the many formal tests and assessments required by government at different points in primary education, commencing from Reception, in the introduction to this publication. He and I are both against this constant, formal testing of children.

Summative Assessment

Most assessments imposed by successive governments are used for summative purposes. Summative assessment is an assessment that gives a score to indicate how well a pupil has performed against the expectation for pupils at that age. It is used by governments to measure schools against other schools and areas against other areas, and by universities and prospective employers to select potential individuals. External tests and examinations are all forms of summative assessment.

Within a school, the same summative assessments may be used to measure pupil against pupil, class against class and progress or otherwise from year to year, for example whether the percentage of pupils achieving at expectation has increased since last year. If these assessments are marked in school or are returned to the school after marking, they may also be used formatively to indicate which areas of teaching need strengthening, because most children failed to achieve well in them.

Formative Assessment

Formative assessment informs teaching and planning. The following are some of the most effective forms of formative assessment for the class teacher:

1. Observation

Watch a child or pair of children closely as they work. How confident are they with the task? If they are not very confident, they may need more practice before moving on. If they have to ask someone else something, is it a small misunderstanding that you can rectify in a conversation or does it need to be re-taught? Is one pupil actually enabling the other to complete the task? If so, the less confident may need more practice or even re-teaching. Are the class more interested in one aspect of the learning than another – should you respond in more detail to that aspect?

2. Conversation

Hold a conversation with a child or pair of children after a taught input and the resulting work is complete. Determine how confident each child is. If not very confident, they may need more practice before moving on. If they cannot answer something or an answer is muddled, is it a small misunderstanding that you can rectify in a conversation or does it need to be re-taught?

3. Explanation

Ask children to explain their working, their thinking or their understanding of an aspect taught. Question them to determine how well they understand, and whether there are gaps in their learning. Ask children to complete a piece of work in any subject, showing all their working, and to explain how they did it and what they learned from it afterwards. Writing reports and explanation texts for an imaginary encyclopaedia can be a very useful form of assessment.

4. Quiz

Following the completion of a week's input or a theme or topic, plan a whole class quiz with questions focusing on the range of knowledge you aimed for the children to retain. Either collect and mark the answers yourself or ask children to mark their own in a different colour pencil or pen. After marking, analyse whether there is/are:

- a pattern in lack of knowledge or misunderstandings, in which case review/re-teach with the whole class. In this case, I would then re-administer the same quiz (having warned the class that you would) and tell them you expect them to beat their own previous score;
- similar gaps in a small number of pupils' knowledge. In this case, teach as a small group; or
- any individuals that need additional input or clarification. Make time to go back through it with the child. It may be useful to re-administer the same quiz two weeks later and a month later to ensure embedding and retention.

5. Essay

Ask the class to write a piece of extended writing (with illustrations if helpful) on the aspect they have studied, after completion of the teaching and associated work. You might give a list of aspects you want included in the piece. Collect and mark yourself, analysing outcomes as with the quizzes.

6. Presentation

Ask children to prepare a PowerPoint presentation about the aspect studied, with a scripted dialogue. If working in pairs, divide the content in half and explain that each child should prepare and script half. Have a series of presentations followed by questions in the last session of the day for a week. Alternatively, ask children to practise and perform a small group role play to retell an incident or an item of learning, such as an episode in a story or an aspect of the life of a famous person, or to present a report to the class on the learning.

It is important to remember that many children can answer questions orally, or in writing, securely soon after the taught input, but may have forgotten it all by the next week. This is because they are functioning on short term memory. If you want children to retain knowledge, they need to use it productively and in different contexts several times, and then the teacher should re-assess a week or more after completion of the work. The learning should be returned to one or two weeks later, with a review and more input. Warm-ups and plenaries to lessons are good times for children to consolidate learning and to reinforce in long term memory. The following can help:

1. Taught input.
2. Discussion and questioning (whole class / small group / paired).
3. Explanation of the main activity.
4. Children complete the main activity.
5. Use the plenary for the children to explain what was done and what they learned.
6. Mark and assess.
7. Open next session with oral review of what was learned in the last lesson.
8. Children prepare a presentation.
9. Watch the presentations.
10. Questions and answers to determine success of learning.
11. Show-you-know walk: children each given a question to ask off their 'secret card' with the answer provided, move round the room and ask each child they meet the question, checking their answer, then answer the other child's question and move on.
12. Plenary: ask the questions off the cards – class 'shout' the answers or tell their partner the answers.
13. Whole class quiz, tell the answers, repeat quiz the next day, tell the answers – repeat as often as needed.
14. Pupils write a report individually, marked by you.

Too many teachers move on through the curriculum too quickly due to the pressures of overload, and as a result many children do not retain the knowledge and understanding they showed at the time of teaching.

Diagnostic Assessment

Formative assessment almost always provides opportunity for diagnostic assessment, and summative assessment often does if the working of difficulties is shown. Diagnostic assessment enables the teacher to not only detect where the pupil is going wrong, but also why they are going wrong – what the misunderstanding is or where there is a gap in the child's learning that needs to be re-taught. This enables the teacher not just to re-teach the whole aspect, but also especially to focus on the misunderstanding and determine why this is happening, so addressing the root of the problem.

Many teachers are using formative assessment diagnostically without realising it, but that underestimates its value and leaves it more to a matter of chance than a planned strategy. The recent trend towards no more marking is particularly worrying as it precludes so many of the valuable opportunities to make a real difference for children. So often a gap in their knowledge can lead to a serious deficiency for years, yet that could have been identified and addressed through quality formative and diagnostic assessment.

As a classroom teacher of almost 30 years, and with regular bouts of classroom practice throughout my years as a consultant (the two most recent being in 2019, both for periods of 12 weeks), I know that it is not possible to move around the classroom having a quality discussion and evaluation of every child's work without setting the class a task that will occupy them for the best part of an hour. At five minutes per pupil, 30 pupils would need 150 minutes or 2 hours 30 minutes, to enable quality, evaluative appraisal of the level of understanding and the errors and gaps addressed through direct conversation.

Marking

For me, taking work home is a crucial part of the job, and as a young teacher I was proud to be in that position of responsibility. I still work on the theory that if a pupil can devote 30 minutes, 45 minutes or even an hour to a piece of work, then I can spend five or six minutes studying and evaluating it. Marking does take longer when you are new to the process and perhaps are unsure about the standards you should expect, but I assure you – the longer you are in the job, the quicker you become.

I firmly believe that teachers should show respect for their pupils' work when marking. I still remember the upset it caused when I received back a piece of extended writing I had put my heart and soul into, to find it covered in red pen focusing on technicalities, and thus degrading my efforts. Consequently, I always mark in black pen and I never write on top of the child's writing. I will put a small, neat line under a word and make a note in the margin: e.g. 'Super sentence opener,' or 'Sp = Wednesday' or a small circle for missing or misused punctuation and 'full stop' in the margin. Sometimes I just put a tick or smiley face in the margin, to show I liked the point I underlined.

Extended writing is widely regarded as the most time consuming and subjective work to assess, particularly in Upper Key Stage 2 and beyond. I can complete a formal assessment of a piece of extended writing of over one side of A4 narrow lined paper (using *The Oxford Writing Criterion Scale, Oxford University Press*) in six minutes or less, including providing feedback, short term targets and advice. As I only recommend this thorough process towards the end of each term (once per term) to track progress and plan forward, I do not consider it a burden, and I get great pleasure from noting the progress made since the previous formal assessment.

For weekly extended writing, I read every child's work and write back to them personally, saying what I enjoyed about it, giving two or three points that are well done or show good progress, and one or two points for development the next week. It normally takes less than five minutes in total. The following is a model of the type of comments I make:

Well done Sammy, I enjoyed this explanation very much, it is clear and well written. I thought you used several really powerful words, I particularly liked 'devastating' and 'consequences'. Next week, please try to use a wider range of sentence openers, including two or three powerful openers.

If I want a significant piece of writing in a subject other than English (which I often do, particularly in science, history and geography), I will ask pupils to do it in the extended writing slot on my timetable, and count that as that subject's time that week rather than as English, so freeing up 45 minutes elsewhere in the week for more creativity. This will then be marked in the same way as the model above. As a result, I am not asking children to write more than one extended piece in a week.

For most other work produced on paper or in books, it is usually sufficient to tick and write a brief comment, such as 'Good effort, Billy' or 'Well tried, Anya'. If there is a misunderstanding or teaching point, for example a repeated error in the way sums are set down in maths or misreading of temperature in science, I will put an example of how it should have been done at the end. Whenever I return marked work to a class, I ask them to read what I have written, together with their work partner, and talk about my comments. They should put up their hand if they do not understand the point I was making, and I will go to them when the class has started work to explain it myself. I always found the children looked forward to receiving marked work back and poured over it together avidly.

Investing in this dialogue with children is an important part of the process of guaranteeing progress and understanding, and I never begrudge the time. Most teachers start their marking in their lunch time and complete it before leaving school at the end of the day. They rarely need to take books home more than once or twice a week. On entry to the profession it may feel time consuming, but practice will bring its rewards, both in speeding up the process, and in the benefits of seeing pupils more motivated and making greater progress.

Standards

As an individual new to teaching, it is important that you are enabled to build up a picture for yourself of what the usual standards are for pupils of the age you teach, and thus what your expectations should be. If this process is not already identified as part of your induction, do not hesitate to ask how and when it will be available. Meanwhile, the following might be helpful in building a secure mental image for your guidance:

- Examine past test papers (SATs) for the end of Key Stages and Year 4.
- Examine previous baseline assessment materials, spelling and grammar papers.
- Examine the end of the previous academic year exercise/workbooks for your class, sent forward with the class by their previous teacher. If this has not been arranged, ask if they are still available – urgently!

- Ask if you may attend any moderation sessions arranged within school or between schools (as an observer), even if they do not involve the year you teach in.
- Discuss the standards of work you should expect with your mentor and with subject leaders, particularly for English, maths and science.
- Check the expectation in your planning against that of other teachers. Where possible, plan with another teacher or team of teachers. Planning is a very good indicator of expectation.
- For any completed work that you are particularly pleased about, discuss with your mentor or the subject leader to achieve an honest appraisal as to whether it is at expectation or above for the child's age and the stage of the academic year.

As the reader will have now realised, most of my teaching career was in schools of significant challenge for one reason or another. Some had a high percentage of pupils new to English, with one establishment being a 450-pupil, brand new school where only six pupils spoke any English at the time of opening. Many posts were overseas in small, isolated, indigenous communities. Many in England were in areas of high poverty and deprivation. Yet one of the most challenging was the final one, a primary school on a very deprived estate on the edge of Kirklees. I taught in Year 6 for three years and was frequently despairing about the pupils' lack of language and inability to construct grammatically correct sentences due to their local accent and dialect. It was the early stages of SATs and I knew that my classes could not attain the standards expected in reading and writing. At that time, the writing was sent away for external marking.

But then, in my third Year 6 class, I discovered Stuart. He was a tall, well-built boy with a calm but humorous disposition, and was hard working and ambitious. He stood a good six inches above any other boy in the school, but then our pupils were mainly small and pale and somewhat puny in build. Stuart excelled at maths, but it was his extended writing that excited me. It was expressive and relevant and usually extremely accurate in spelling, grammar and punctuation. I was so excited that I passed his work round in staff meetings, with very little approval shown by my colleagues. They probably felt that my despair at the usual standards I saw was a reflection on their teaching in previous years, which it wasn't – it was a reflection on the vulnerability of the community the children were growing up in. But now I was teaching Stuart, a boy with significant gifts, who was to excel above all others across the region.

Eventually, I became the advisor for assessment for Kirklees, and in that role, I travelled round the 150 primary schools in the local authority, auditing the implementation of SATs and moderating standards. This work took me to the most deprived areas and to the most affluent – and that was what caused me the biggest and most rapid learning curve. In the more affluent suburbs and villages, the extended writing was not only equally as good as Stuart's – it actually frequently surpassed his. When compared with pupils across the whole country, Stuart's achievements – significant as they were in my previous school – were purely 'average'!

This exemplifies why having a thorough working understanding of what pupils of the age you teach are capable of achieving is essential for all teachers. Prior to my local authority work, I only had a mental picture of achievement in the types of schools I worked in. I assumed the best I saw was the best. When I was exposed to a much wider range of backgrounds, I discovered I had never met 'the best' before.

I also discovered that Stuart was just an eleven year old of *average* height!

My Top Tips for Marking and Assessment

- Study the standards achieved by children of the age you teach.
- Marking and feedback are both important, although all work may not need to be marked (especially not always in the foundation subjects) if formative assessment has been achieved in other ways. Remember, it is valued by children – so do it with pride.
- Ask pupils to discuss your marking and comments in pairs.
- Listen to children and watch them work.
- Diagnose the problem when a child or group constantly make the same errors.

CHAPTER 14

Policy into Practice

When I first started teaching in England in 1965, schools did not have policies, only rules. When I returned from the Caribbean in late 1986, most schools had written policies, although many teachers did not seem to know what they were. Since the introduction of Ofsted in 1993, policies and how well they are interpreted have become very important in schools.

When schools are first developing a new policy, they are usually inclusive during the process, consulting the leadership team, the governing body, often other headteacher colleagues and sometimes the wider staff. The process invariably involves much discussion and debate, sensitivity and inclusion – policies are not arrived at lightly. The point of a policy is that all staff conduct the school day, approaches, management and behaviours in a similar way – which aspires to be the best way for the children and community the school serves. There is no point in a policy if it is not reflected in daily practice by all.

Staff joining a school with existing policies can have no say in their principles; it is incumbent upon new teachers to conform to existing policies rather than to be a maverick. Initially, there should be a genuine effort to implement all school policies in their full and intended meaning. As part of a newly appointed teacher's induction, their mentor or a senior leader should discuss the policies with them and answer any questions, whilst explaining any areas the new teacher may not fully understand. However, that does not mean that a teacher new to the school should not question and challenge policies once they have made a serious effort to implement in full over time, or if they feel a policy causes real offence.

The following are the options if any policy is unworkable or distasteful to a teacher after making a serious attempt to understand and implement it. Discuss the policy with your mentor, year leader, or a member of the leadership team. Check that you are interpreting the policy correctly. Be very clear about a) the steps and effort you have made to make the policy effective for your class, and b) precisely which aspects of the policy cause you difficulties and why, with examples if appropriate.

1. Ask for an opportunity to raise the policy in a staff meeting for whole staff discussion, and guidance on how others interpret and implement the policy. Do remember that you may be misinterpreting the policy and that is why it seems unworkable (at least in part) to you. Be aware that this request may not be granted, but be assured that it will usually lead to discussion and review within the leadership team.

2. Become a closet grumbler – find like-minded staff and mutter in corners. *This is the worst thing you can do*, and it does you no favours in a professional sense. Schools have strong networks and communication channels, and the worst thing that can happen to you is to have a label such as 'difficult' pinned to you. Closet grumbling or moaning is unprofessional and destructive in a school.

If there is a policy that truly offends your principles, and if all efforts to discuss this and come to a compromise have failed, you may have to start considering a change of schools. This is a drastic action and should not be needed, thankfully, if step 1 has been successfully implemented. If the policy is so offensive to you that you cannot bear to continue to subscribe to it, and all efforts at negotiation have failed, you may have to consider this step. However, do be aware that, when reading CVs and applications for posts, one of the important considerations made by leadership is the applicant's record of employment. Professionals who repeatedly spend very short periods of time in placements (and are not supply teaching) will usually be less favourably regarded than those who spend three years or more in each post.

You could consider consulting your teachers' union for advice. This can also be controversial and may offend leadership. No school wants a negative relationship with the unions, and some may resent the involvement of an outside body. Better to only seek a discreet and confidential consultation with the union representative for advice and guidance only, if all else has failed.

You could also consider consulting the chair of governors for advice. Be aware this may well have a similar effect to talking to a union. Most leadership teams and governing bodies have a strong professional, working relationship with all wanting what is best for the school and the team. The governors will have read and approved the policies and may react adversely to you questioning them or the head, and leadership may see this as you going behind their backs. Thus, again, if you need to resort to this – having tried all possible negotiation yourself – ask for a confidential meeting for advice with the governor best positioned to speak on policy.

Your mindset needs to be not that you seek to undermine or change school policy, but rather to understand it better – to understand how and why it was deemed necessary and to learn how you can implement it more effectively, so that it does work for you and your class. In the rare event that a policy is actually flawed, for example in an assessment policy, a policy for children with EAL or a diversity policy, there may be something you personally find unacceptable. If the policy under question is a non-negotiable in school, you may need to consider looking for a new position and make that principle a key question you ask at the close of an interview, when candidates are invariably asked if they have any questions. This will ensure that you will be joining a school with a differing stance.

The Importance of Policies to a School

In 1999, I had the huge privilege of being asked to relocate to Qatar, in order to do a 'start up' with my good friend and former colleague from my last full-time teaching position in the Kirklees primary school. He had been appointed as the founding principal of a school that did not yet exist in a remote community, a 50-minute drive across the desert from the capital city of Doha. The school was founded to educate the children of the 5,000 employees (now over 35,000) of two major off-shore gas companies. The children had previously been bused across the desert to schools in Doha.

In order for the start up to be as authentic as it should be, we did not tell the incoming staff that I was in post as a consultant on a limited contract and I worked under the title of being my colleague's deputy principal and head of primary. We were opening the primary school first and then building the secondary, year by year, as pupils left the primary phase.

Prior to the school opening, I had six months to write the whole school curriculum and all the policies, whilst still in post with Kirklees as an advisor until the end of the academic year. Everything I wrote was sent to the principal, we discussed them and signed them off as draft for the first year of the new school. In my consultant role, I had very much been part of advising and auditing primary policies across the 150 primary schools in Kirklees; I had already designed and co-designed curricula that had become highly sought after and well regarded, so this was work I enjoyed and put considerable time and effort into.

All the newly appointed teaching staff arrived in the community over two weeks prior to the opening of the new school, and we devoted two full weeks to induction, introductions, team building, policy review and discussion, systems analysis and so forth. There were 45 primary classroom generalist and specialist teachers at the time of opening, and at the start of our second year of operation there were 60.

We opened in September 1999 with 450 children of predominantly Middle and Far Eastern nationalities. Only six children were European/English and only nine children were English speaking at the time of opening. The vast majority of the children were from the homes of the men who did the daily manual labour on the gas sites or in the community, and these children had very diverse prior educational experiences in their first language. Some, such as those from isolated communities in countries like Nepal and Bangladesh, had little education at all. There were 45 languages in the school by the end of the first year and over 65 in the second year.

We deliberately did not develop a great raft of policies, and all our policies had been developed with these facts about our diverse starting points for the children in mind. Almost all the teaching staff were from European, United Kingdom or Australian backgrounds, but we were extremely lucky to have a large and highly talented pool of support assistants formed from the wives in the community (who were not allowed to work outside the community), who were mainly multi-lingual and a great strength to the school.

We were not believers in lengthy policies to impress, the first key fundamental respect policy could encompass almost everything that could arise in the school year:

- Respect all adults in the school: listen carefully when spoken to, do as you are asked to do when you are asked to do it and to the best of your ability, and reply to questions politely.
- Respect all other children: listen when they are talking to you, help when you are able to, show care and responsibility when they are near and offer friendship and support when you can.
- Respect the school buildings and their contents: move around school in such a way that you cannot cause damage or harm, make way courteously for anyone you meet and never run inside the buildings.

Our three most important policies, however, were never put under one header and were top of our list of non-negotiables in the first year of the school. This was because they were key to drawing our diverse population together, and to enable all to develop their understanding and ability to speak in English rapidly and with confidence.

- The Talk Policy: all children were to be allowed to talk quietly at all times in lessons, switching constantly between first language and emerging English, providing the teacher was not talking to the child or the whole class at that time. The only exceptions were during extended writing after the first term and when an assessment exercise was being undertaken that required the teacher to know what a child could do when unsupported.
- The No Shouting Policy: no adult was ever to raise their voice at a child or children except during outdoor PE and swimming when necessary, or in a sudden emergency. All adults should speak to all children with warmth and respect, making eye contact and with a smile as appropriate.
- The Open Door Policy: no classroom door should ever be closed, unless advised by year leaders due to weather conditions or a sandstorm.

The open door policy was to enable monitoring of both the talk and the no shouting policies. For the two years I was at the school, I walked the entire buildings at least once a day, and often twice a day, at no set times. Rather than opening a door, making an entrance and potentially disturbing the class, I preferred to pause in the open doorway, watching and listening, asking myself:

- Are the children busy, engaged and happy looking?
- Are the children talking to each other, switching languages as appropriate, providing the teacher is not talking directly to them or the whole class?
- Is the teacher interacting with children with a warm and open manner?

Naturally, I enjoyed the many snapshots of learning I gleaned from these walkabouts, but my priorities were the implementation of the three policies we knew would enable the most rapid settling in, establishing of relationships and learning of English as a common language.

In the United Kingdom, we say it takes up to five years to become confident in English, and it can be up to ten years to be fully competent. In the second year of that school, every child who had started the school at the beginning of Year 5 and was now in Year 6, took the English SATs and they were posted back to England for marking by the English school markers. 100% of the children achieved the age expectation of the time – a Level 4 in extended writing in English - and half achieved a Level 5.

Yet despite the constant daily evidence of the impact and effectiveness of these three policies, there were just two members of the teaching team (who had become friends since arriving) who were unable to conform. They would close their classroom doors (which did not have a glass panel in) and when I entered I would frequently find the children working in silence (copying from a whiteboard much of the time) and the teachers seated behind their desks. After two years of attempting to reform their opinions and attitudes, it was agreed that the two teachers should not have their contracts renewed.

Interestingly, the stronger of the two personalities had also become the leader of a very small but vociferous group of staffroom grumblers and moaners, a practice that mainly disappeared as soon as they had left. We felt unhappy that our best efforts to integrate these two colleagues had failed, although the remaining 43 were very content with the school, and HMI judged it to be outstanding.

My Top Tips for Policy into Practice

- Study the school policies and be sure you are interpreting them as intended.
- Implement school policies to the very best of your ability.
- Do seek help if you have difficulty interpreting or implementing a policy.
- Do consult leadership if you have personal difficulty with underlying principles in a policy.
- Avoid bringing outside agencies into the discussions unless absolutely desperate.
- Avoid involving the governors unless advised to by leadership or – as a last resort – to have a confidential consultation for advice.
- Apply for new jobs if you find you cannot agree with important policies after a reasonable period.
- Establish your personal red lines and ask about them at interview.
- Avoid becoming a moaner/grumbler within school.

CHAPTER 15

Diversity

I have left this – one of the most important issues in the book – to last because I do not know how to tackle it. I am afraid of writing about prejudice and abuse, I am scared of offending people I care so much about. But it is people like me, perhaps, who, by our silence and avoidance, have allowed bigotry and bias to perpetuate the prejudices of others, and make the lives of so many at least unhappy and at worst horrific.

It alarms me to say that I never met or knew a person of another ethnicity until I went overseas in 1970, aged 26. How could that be? I went through 14 years of schooling and three years of higher education without ever seeing anyone of any ethnicity other than indigenous white pupils and teachers. Also, my initial five and a half years of teaching were in two schools with no ethnicity other than white British amongst pupils or staff. I was an ignorant novice.

In 1970, my ex-husband and I relocated to the Bahamas, where we lived and worked for five years in a small community of 1,500 black Bahamians. There was only one other white person, an American Roman Catholic priest who was 74 years old and lived by the church two miles from our cottage and the school. We taught in an all-age school of 250 pupils, aged four to 17 (and older – we suspected), with every one of them black Bahamian, every member of staff black Bahamian and with a black Bajan headteacher.

I gave birth to my two children while we were there, in a hospital 36 miles from our 'settlement', as the communities were called in those days. The entire staff of the hospital were black, and every patient was black except me. In all those years and in all my interactions, I never met any racial prejudice and we built strong professional relationships – except in the hospital, where some of the nursing staff (but none of the doctors) were quite unpleasant towards me.

From 1979 to 1986 we lived on a tiny island called Cayman Brac in the Caribbean, just 12 miles long and one mile wide. My two best friends on that island were a black Trinidadian called Maurice, who was hilarious and talented and the best of company, and a black Bajan (from Barbados) called Peter, who was highly intelligent and articulate and – after a couple of beers – very angry about the history of black Africans in the Caribbean and Americas. I loved both of these men as friends, but I also had many other good friends of similar ethnicities around the Caribbean – Trevor and Janice and Sue and Bobby and Shirley and so on. In all the years I was there, I only had two close white friends.

I never ever thought about diversity or race, except when Peter pushed me into an argument when I would plead the horrors of history and changing times to avoid a real fracas. Both in the Bahamas and the Cayman Islands, one of my specialist subjects was West Indian history, which I taught to GCSE level in the Bahamas. In fact, I actually took the subject myself – with the students – so adding to my personal portfolio. In preparing to teach this subject, about which I knew nothing initially, I studied the whole history of discovery, invasion, piracy, privateers, slavery and colonisation in considerable detail – which was not easy in those days, before the internet.

The horrors of slavery and 'The Middle Passage' (the journey from Africa to the 'New World' by primitive sailing ship), where over half the incarcerated Africans chained in the hold died and were thrown overboard, remain with me until today.

Much of my teaching career was in schools with between 60% and 100% pupils of ethnicities other than white European, and I loved teaching these pupils and highly respected their parents, my colleagues and the communities within which I worked. The greatest challenges I faced in teaching were with poor white children from areas of great deprivation and with huge conflict in their lives.

For three years in the early 2000s, I took the role of primary strategy manager in Education Bradford, a post which gave me the privilege of access to the entire data for the city of Bradford and its surrounding communities. I can state unequivocally that – in a city of considerable ethnic mix and with the largest Pakistani community in England – amongst those ethnicities and cultures, the largest underperforming group statistically was poor white boys.

For five years, I taught in a middle school with 60% of the pupils being of Asian origin and 40% being poor white. The children of Asian origin were a delight to teach – hard working and motivated with parents who cared and wanted their children to succeed. It was the children from the poor white homes, mainly based in one large council estate, who caused teachers the greatest difficulties and resisted our best efforts to integrate them and to change their life opportunities. They couldn't, in the main, see the point of education!

So now you see why I have avoided this chapter. My personal experiences in no way resemble the terrible prejudices I am well aware go on around me. The prejudices I have experienced in my life have all been inflicted by white people.

Throughout my career, I felt a lack of opportunity or recognition as a woman, and frequently saw men promoted above me for whom I had little regard as teachers. In the years prior to 1990, it was fully accepted that a young man could often get promotions and become a headteacher at least ten years before a woman, even though the percentage of women in teaching in primary schools far outstripped men.

Thus, perhaps the reader can see why I feel under qualified to talk about diversity. I truly see no ethnic divide and believe that every child in every class should be treated as a person in their own right, with respect and a high regard for their potential. The most able children I have taught have not been indigenous white British. The most amazing pupils I ever taught were of Asian origin in Bradford and of Middle and Far Eastern ethnicities in Qatar. How sad it is that politics and changing governments led to the abandoning of the most visionary phrase a conservative government of the time ever gave to education: Every Child Matters.

The most repugnant phrase that is so often heard is:
'I'm not prejudiced, but...'

When issues of diversity or prejudice arise, listen carefully and be prepared to learn and be flexible in your opinions. Accept that you may not always know the right answers – but the worst thing to do is nothing. The following is a very wise saying about differing opinions which has been with me for many years:
'No matter how thin you slice the onion there are still two sides.'

The Curriculum

Ensure that you build issues and people that reflect the diversity of the world into your medium and short term planning of the existing school curriculum. The following are just a few examples:

- If you are planning a unit for a place in geography, include positive study of ethnicity and culture.
- If you are planning a unit for ecology in geography or science, include people from a range of ethnicities and cultures doing great works around the world.
- If you are planning a unit for a period of history, include focus on human rights of the time, diversity and famous characters from a range of cultures.
- If you are planning a unit for science on any aspect, ensure it reflects great works or discoveries by scientists of different ethnicities and cultures.
- If you are planning a unit that includes the work of famous artists in art or music, ensure you include diverse ethnicities and cultures

When planning your curriculum for diversity, particularly reflect the ethnicities reflected in your class or in the community the school serves. Be proactive in acknowledging diversity to the class, ever promoting a fully integrated and respectful society.

This is a chapter of the book that might have been better written by someone else, so I refer readers back to Halil Tamgumus' contribution in the introduction, in case any readers missed it.

My Top Tips for Diversity

- Every Child Matters.
- Make every child feel valued and important.
- Seek out the quiet child and build their esteem.
- Seek out the angry child and build their esteem.
- Seek out the isolated child and build their esteem.
- Develop a culture of inclusion where every child does matter and is valued.
- Embrace all cultures represented in the school.
- Ensure that, within your teaching, diverse ethnicities and cultures are promoted and celebrated.

CHAPTER 16

Case Studies

I am particularly proud of this section of the publication which includes case studies from friends and colleagues across the spectrum of the profession. They have told their diverse stories with a deep sincerity and respect for all, and often with humour, yet there are common threads throughout that show a consistency and commitment that makes our profession one of the greatest in the world.

These stories are presented in alphabetical order by surname.

Go with the Flow by Sara Alston

When I started teaching back in 1986, it was a different world. We took the children to the park to draw (and hug) trees on the spur of the moment because it was a sunny day. There were no risk assessments then. Without the National Curriculum, we could choose and direct the children's learning according to their (and our) interests. In my second term, we did an extended unit on measurement. We measured everything in sight from the tables to the headteacher! We collected measurements of different animals and laid them out in tape on the floor to compare. To finish the unit, we created a life-sized papier mâché albatross which was hoisted up to the hall ceiling. It was still hanging there when I visited the school four years later as an advisory teacher.

Teaching was fun and flexible thirty years ago; it is up to us as a profession to make it that way again. We were able to respond to children's needs which promoted their sense of belonging and engagement. We were able to adapt and respond to children's interests and return to or continue learning to ensure it was embedded.

As we move forward, we need to ensure that this flexibility is combined with rigour to create a curriculum that is truly broad, enriching and engaging to meet a range of children's needs. We must adapt the curriculum to meet the children's needs, not expect the children to change to suit what and how we are teaching.

Sara Alston
Consultant and Trainer: SEA Inclusion and Safeguarding

A Genius Music Lesson – Or Not! by Humaira Batool

'And you will be observed teaching a music lesson,' stated my headteacher, like it was the most ordinary ask. Music? My heart sank. I was expecting to teach something normal like maths or English. Not music! I had successfully avoided attending three quarters of my music lectures at university... the lecturer had actually once caught me walking off in the direction of the library because an essay was due to be handed in.

Being a person who loves a challenge, I mustered up my NQT+1 energy and started gathering resources. Then I had a lightbulb moment: a poem, entitled 'Gran, can you rap?' I was going to teach my class of Year 4s to rap. Yes, to rap, with some wise teacher person from the council observing me. What could go wrong?

The observed lesson was straight after break. I skipped along to the female W.C. and changed into a far too big hoodie and some jogging pants. My then husband wouldn't lend me his gold chain! As a class, we capitalised on the literacy link... discussing the poem and its meaning. In the end I proceeded to rap the poem out, complete with rap artist gestures, whilst a very prim and proper, middle-aged gentleman in a crisp suit sat at the back. Silently. He scribbled away. And carried on scribbling.

The twenty minutes that I had expected him to stay for turned into half an hour. No sign of him leaving. He stayed until the very end of the lesson, the last fifteen minutes of which comprised of me sweating under the thick hoodie, my class losing interest because they really didn't want to sing that song for what felt like the 50th time.

I expected my feedback to comment on my wonderful attire, my engaging rap and the fact I had put on a good show. Instead, it went something like this: The lesson requires improvement. Consider planning some additional activities. I think what he meant was... how long did you expect them to sing their hearts out for?

I acted upon the feedback! A few years of intense CPD later, I was appointed assistant head of the very same three-form entry primary school. The moral of the story is: decide what the key ingredient of your lesson is, what do you actually want the children to learn? Then plan from that, as opposed to putting on a show.

Humaira Batool
Associate Assistant Principal

And Having the Last Laugh... by Ginny Bootman

My NQT year was a very interesting time in my life. Even the run up to becoming an NQT was not without its own trials and tribulations. It was 1993 and there were far more teachers wanting jobs than there were actual jobs. I remember once finding out that 300 people had applied for one particular position. I must have literally applied for over 30 teaching jobs. I often didn't even get a reply to my application, never mind an interview. The clock was ticking ever closer to summer holidays.

I was training in Liverpool and applying for jobs in the city, on the Wirral. I even took a ferry across the Mersey to attend an interview. It was a crazy time. Once, I had to be in Liverpool and Chester on the same day for interviews and my wonderful mum was going to pay for a taxi to get me from one interview to the next one. I remember being at a railway station crying my eyes out because I had been turned down for yet another job. My poor mum gave me sympathy down the phone and just kept on saying keep going...

Confused and somewhat irritated, I even rang up one of the schools to ask why I had not been short listed. Their reply has stayed with me to this day:

'We had over 300 applications so the head sat us down and asked us over a cup of tea what extra skill we would like the new teacher to have that wasn't already on the job specification. The consensus was someone who could play the piano. You obviously do not fit that category, so your application went in the bin.' (My handwritten application which had taken hours of blood, sweat and tears went in the bin because of a decision made over a cuppa)

Fast forward to the second to last week of the summer term. My home was in North Yorkshire and I had gone home to fester, rejected and disheartened. I saw a job advertised in Gateshead. I'd never been there, didn't really know where it was but in for a penny in for a pound! I had no car, so my wonderful brother chauffeured me to my interview. As soon as I arrived, I asked how long I'd be as my brother was going to pop to The Metro Centre and needed to know what time to return. (Yes, it was before the time that mobile phones were invented). The look of horror on the headteacher's face didn't bode well for the rest of the day...

So I had my interview. There were five candidates and we all had to wait in the staffroom and were called up one by one to be interviewed and then returned tight lipped as to what had been discussed in 'that room'. Thinking about it, the experience was not dissimilar to The Apprentice. One candidate was full of it, saying he had the job in the bag because he played the tuba and so did the headteacher. I was slightly crestfallen but pleased for him and was wondering how much piano lessons would be... LOL!

And then – behold the ceremonial walking in of the headteacher to invite the successful candidate back into the office happened. I could hear the tuba duet playing in my head and see them skipping off happily into the distance playing 'The Floral Dance', with me wondering what gems my brother had bought from The Metro Centre and my mother ready with a box of tissues. Suddenly, my name echoed through the air. Tuba Man looked like he was going to ask for a recount and so began my teaching career in Gateshead...

My first experience of meeting the staff was at the end of year staff do. A lovely teaching assistant took me under her wing and offered me a room for the night and actually offered me bed and lodgings if I needed it. So far, so good.

Then came the wrath of the former PE co-ordinator. I naively thought that this individual had happily swapped from PE co-ordinator to maths. It soon became apparent that this move in subject management was as a result of a fly away comment which had been scooped up by the headteacher and actioned swiftly. There was bad feeling, which came my way by association...

I visited my classroom. Mr maths co-ordinator's first words were 'The locusts have been...' I looked confused. He carried on... 'This cupboard should be full, but they've all emptied it.' And so his unfounded dislike of me continued. I remember one day in a crowded staffroom he said:
'I bet she doesn't know the offside rule'

That night I enrolled in evening school to become a qualified football referee. Needless to say, once I qualified, I knew more than he did about the offside rule... Boom! Back of the net!

During my first year as an NQT in the early 1990s in inner-city Gateshead, having been given the gift of the role of PE co-ordinator, my first sports day arrived. I had organised it with amazing precision. Nothing could go wrong. How wrong could I be? The beanbag race approached. I noticed in the corner of my eye that one of the boys from my class was still wearing his hoop earrings. I politely asked him to remove them for fear of him catching them whilst retrieving the aforementioned beanbags. Next thing I know, lo and behold a very tall, very stocky and angry, bare-chested man approached me with malice. He reliably informed me in front of a packed athletic track via a broad Geordie-shouted-accent:
'I div na think that mi son is tekkin out his ear ring!'

I did the only thing an NQT would do in that situation... I walked with purpose towards my headteacher and quietly said:
'I'm handing this one over to you..'

My newfound father-friend from sports day reared his head again later in the year... Rather intoxicated, he found his way into the school after school had finished and was using foul language – very inappropriate for an educational establishment. The senior manager had rather coincidentally hidden himself away in his classroom at this point and so I happened upon a conversation between the aforementioned father and a rather wound up

cleaner. She asked him to curb his language to which he replied:
'I div na think you are a teacher and only one of them lot can tell me what to do!'

At which point I emerged from my classroom as a vision, and said in a somewhat authoritarian voice:
'I am a teacher and I am asking you to stop using this abusive language.'
To which he replied:
'Ok then, hinny,' and pootled off quite happily. I had no plan B...

You never know what will happen as an NQT, and so it happened to me one autumn day. My Reception children were happily playing in our classroom. The next minute, I heard a noise and smelt a dreadful smell. A huge, rabid looking Alsatian type of dog launched itself in through the classroom window into the middle of a classroom full of unsuspecting four year olds.

To add insult to injury, this creature had somehow brought in what smelt like the entire contents of a sewer! I became lion tamer crossed with Mary Poppins and quickly and quietly told the children we were going to the hall to do 'something lovely', whilst fending off sewage-creature with a metre stick.

As we passed the headteacher's office I reliably informed him, 'I'm handing this one over to you.'

Ginny Bootman
Senco

Flying Through Space by Alex Caunt

It was my first term as an NQT. I'd had a horrific first half term but after the October holiday I really found my groove and confidence. It was a mid-topic lesson about space; I was showing the kids a video about Buzz Aldrin and Neil Armstrong – and I was getting quite excited – feeling smug. The video is coming on and I know they will love the lesson. So, I climbed onto the side cupboards in the classroom to bask in their enjoyment...

Little did I realise that the window was unfastened and as I leant back, smiling and feeling cocky, the window opened right out and I literally fell backwards straight out of the window – proper Del Boy style – and landed on the concrete back path that led to the field. Time kind of slowed down before 32 Year 5s rushed to the window and then out of the back door to find me crumpled in a heap on the floor, rubbing my head!

Safe to say, no more work was done that afternoon, and during the three more years spent in that classroom, I never sat on the side again!

Alex Caunt
Class Teacher

Finding My Teacher Presence by Sharon Day

I started teaching in 1984. I found it hard to find my teacher voice – my teacher presence. Even though it is important to be authentic as a teacher, it is also important to not just be yourself; some things have to be hidden and protected. So, what to do? I decided to channel my favourite teacher. She was Miss Denise Warren from Wrose Junior School and she taught me when I was top juniors (now known as Year 6). She was the sort of teacher that ensured you learned the facts you needed (because of her, I have always known all my times tables), but she also allowed for expression and self-study (I remember doing a whole project on Gladys Aylward because I had been inspired the previous weekend at home by the film starring Ingrid Bergman).

Miss Warren was firm, fair and friendly. She listened to us and heard us. I became her. This became my style of teaching too, until it felt natural to work in this way. I think it is important to find inspiration and to use experience to shape who you are. Miss Warren inspired me. I hope that I have done the same for children that I have taught through the years.

Sharon Day
Mathematics Consultant: Primary and EYFS

The Importance of the People Around You and the Culture of the School by Joshua Denton-Collins

There is no other way of saying it, my NQT year started unusually. Day two of my teaching career, and I found myself, my partner teacher (who was also new to the school), the headteacher and the chair of governors in a pitch-black forest trying to find the place where 60 children from our school were camping. Luckily for everyone, we stumbled upon the camp fairly quickly and found everyone was present and correct around the campfire with the other members of staff and the forest experts.

Whilst this 48-hour trip did exactly what it was designed to do, build a relationship between new adults and children and develop a team spirit between pupils, perhaps one of the most significant things that happened for me was the forming of relationships with the other staff. Struggling to sleep, we shared funny stories, terrifying teaching experiences and visions for the future of the school.

Upon arrival back at school, smelly, wet and most of all completely shattered, we had another three hours to face before pick-up time. Before we stepped in the school, however, two teaching assistants had placed cups of tea into our hands, a teacher had taken the children outside to play and we were told to sit down whilst the kitchen staff brought us lunch fresh from the kitchen. The place was just filled with love, friendship, and support from everyone.

Over the coming weeks and months, these relationships were cemented and became absolutely fundamental to the development of my teaching practice. Within a couple of terms, I knew exactly who to turn to when I needed help and the school had an incredibly strong culture of everyone pitching in. If I had an issue with supporting a child with SEND, I knew I could pop down the corridor and speak to Miss P about how she supported them last year. Should I need an idea for a topic or community outcome, I would stick my head in next door and chat to Mr K. When I was unsure about how I was teaching reading, I simply asked the head to pop in for five minutes and coach me.

We would spend five minutes every morning chatting through what we had planned for the day as a staff team. On Friday mornings, we shared breakfast together and on Friday evenings we visited the pub, bonding socially. Since leaving the school and moving across the country, this school culture and ethos around coaching, supporting, and developing its staff is still something I am searching for and trying to instil in my current school.

Have I developed my practice significantly since then? Absolutely! Am I a better teacher today than I was at the commencement of my career? You bet! However, without those relationships and leaders at the start of my career, I would be nowhere near the teacher I am today with the values and ideas I uphold within the classroom. As I start to take my first tentative steps into leadership, I hope that one day I manage to emulate the culture I found at my first school.

Joshua Denton-Collins
Class Teacher/Co-ordinator

Two Examples from My Experience of Plunging into Teaching by Rachel Gregson

Example 1

Having rehearsed all the songs and dances for the Christmas Nativity with nearly 90 young children, what could possibly go wrong on the day? Well, I played the piano piece too early which confused all of the children and they started to sing the wrong song. I had to quickly find the next page; however all the music fell off the piano and I just had to improvise. Ten children in groups of two were meant to skip down the centre of the aisle, however only one pair set off and the others did not follow. Everyone did manage to muddle through, however, and it was a great performance.

Example 2

One day in the middle of a maths lesson, a child started screaming and running around the classroom because their tooth was 'about' to fall out. As I was explaining to the children what fractions were, the child ran over to me and explained that his tooth had fallen out.

I then said, 'Where is the tooth now?'

The whole class erupted into laughter as the tooth fell out of his mouth, went down my leg and onto my shoe. Trying to calm the children down was quite challenging as they were more interested in telling tooth jokes:
'What did the judge say to the dentist? Do you swear to pull the tooth, the whole tooth and nothing but the tooth?'
'Use your own toothbrush!' he bristled.

I definitely learned during this incident that you cannot predict what is going to happen in the classroom.

Rachel Gregson
Class Teacher at the end of her second year in teaching

Trip Up! by Sam Keys

In my first year of primary teaching, I went on a trip to Germany with a group of Year 6 children. We were visiting our partner school. On the second evening, we took part in a fantastic parade which eventually led to a huge bonfire in front of a grand stage where several thousand locals were celebrating.

The mayor of the town was addressing the crowd in German, when all of a sudden the crowd turned to us and we were ushered onto the stage. The mayor spoke and turned to us. My colleague pushed me forward and I was handed a microphone... Only speaking basic German, I was terrified.

To this day, I still don't know what I said, and I cringe so much thinking about it. The crowd laughed and cheered (I think!) so it can't have been too bad!

A little later...

As a young-looking NQT, we were on a school trip to just outside of Leeds when our bus broke down on the motorway. We quickly got all of the children to safety at the side of the road and the bus driver made some calls. A few minutes later, the highways agency and police turned up. I walked towards them to explain the situation and the officer shouted 'Son, get back! Please go and get your teacher!' The officer refused to believe that I wasn't a pupil!

It is a relief that there is better support and mentoring for NQTs today, but you may still find yourselves wrong-footed from time to time. Don't be afraid to refer such situations to a more experienced colleague if you feel uncertain of procedure.

Sam Keys
Deputy Headteacher

'I've Not Even Taken the Register Yet!' by Steve Ladd

There I was, primed and ready to launch my career. I'd trained for four years for this moment. Interview, staff introductions and INSET had gone well, but we all know that it's the impression you make with the students that matters. I was a fresh-faced (and what I really mean was that I didn't need to trouble with my razor too much), NQT PE teacher, but had been given a Year 10 tutor group. 'There's a lot of rugby lads in that group, so we thought you'd get along just fine,' I was informed.

Confidently, I marched up to the temporary hut that had been there for 15 years, and made my way through the group of rather large students gathered outside. So far, so good. Brandishing my less than polished teacher look, and ignoring the mutterings from those on the edge, I proudly picked through my new bunch of PE teacher keys, selected the one with the purple plastic fob (purple for pastoral) and started to unlock the door, thinking I'm smashing this! The lock didn't move. I tried again. Still the lock didn't move. An uncomfortable feeling stirred in my stomach and I could sense the deepening redness of my face as I struggled to maintain my calm.

The mutterings from the edge grew louder, resembling giggling. Do I perform the walk of shame to try and find someone or stay and supervise my new tutor group, who are quickly losing patience? In a desperate act of survival and self-deprecation, I mocked my inauspicious introduction to the group.

How would they respond to this? Thankfully, it worked, and they started to suggest who might help.

As I pondered my next move, my heroine rode into town. The part-time maths teacher, who taught in this hut on Thursdays and Fridays, had arrived to drop off some books. She had the magic key, and as we entered what was to be our tutor room for the following two years, a new thought ran through my head: had I picked up the register?

Steve Ladd
PE and English Teacher, Danesfield Church of England School

How Things Have Changed! by Hayley McDonnell

I entered the A-level classroom in a grammar school, as an NQT in 1998. You could – back then. I taught classes in every year group, two lots of GCSE groups and two lots of A-level groups. I was also a form tutor. In at the deep end!

I was not expected to teach a lesson during interview. I was trusted to teach, plan, assess and everything else in between. I took my position seriously and didn't let my students down. I was nervous as hell teaching my first A-level lesson with no one observing me, but I never let it show. Slowly, I found my groove and settled into my own creative, effective flow of teaching. I loved it, felt supported and respected, and wanted to do well for myself and my students.

I moved on five years later to another grammar school for 16 years... I've trained teachers over the years and the expectations for them are so different. It's so cookie cutter now. My last post was a maternity humanities post and there was no specialist knowledge required... all pre-prepared PowerPoints and resources. No creativity needed or allowed.

The profession needs to find a midway point, with the creativity and freedoms I experienced in my early years in the profession counterbalanced by the accountability required today.

Hayley McDonnell
PD/SMSC consultant

Planning to Excite by Katy McCullough

If you are bored planning a lesson, then the children will be bored taking part in the lesson. If an idea, concept or activity excites you, then it will excite the kids too... even the ones who like to eat the resources!

My best lessons have been the ones I have been excited about teaching and my worst have been the ones I found tedious and uninspiring to plan (and all too often those were the 'special lessons' I had planned in meticulous detail in a bid to impress someone). Children don't naturally talk about what they learned in school today, they talk about what they *did*.

Although teachers talk about learning objectives – and quite rightly use these to plan for progression and breadth and to help children to understand the point of what they are doing – what the children are really interested in is the activity – what they did. No one remembers the day they first used speech marks correctly to punctuate direct speech in a paragraph of text. Everyone remembers the day the whole class went outside and shouted at each other from opposite sides of the playground and then wrote down what their partner had yelled, using speech marks of course!

Establish the learning objectives and then spend your planning time working out a way to bring them alive. If you are excited about the lesson you are about to teach and the activities you have planned then the children will sense that and respond to it, they will want to be involved in the learning you are doing together and they will be motivated to listen carefully, understand and improve. Learning is so much easier when everyone is enjoying what they are doing and so much harder when everyone is bored.

I would also say that it is so important to harness enthusiasm and grasp learning opportunities when they occur. Some of my best lessons have been when something unexpected has happened, either in the children's response to material or just in general, and instead of sticking rigidly to the lesson plan I have had the confidence to explore off the beaten track for a bit.

Lesson objectives do not have to be set in stone, they can be added to and reviewed in the plenary then returned to in a future lesson. What's more important is to enjoy learning and to value where the children want to take their learning, and also to remember that teaching is an organic, relational process that can't always be pre-specified.

Learning objectives help us to do our job well but they do not tell us what our job is – they are a tool and not a cage!

Katy McCullough
Pupil Premium Champion and Year 6 teacher

Early Teaching Memories: Feeling the Heat! by Tamsin Nellist

First day of my teaching career, I was so nervous… it was January, snowing, and I was going to a totally different building because of a shared training event. Of course, I got lost down a winding Welsh country lane with no phone reception. A dog walker saw me and offered his help, he offered to drive my car to the main road and suggested that I could follow it round and meet him, bringing his dog.

I thanked him profusely, so grateful that he'd stopped. As I saw my shiny Golf accelerate away, I stood in a snow storm in the middle of nowhere. With no phone reception and a dog on a shabby lead whose name I didn't know, I wondered how I would explain this to my new employer – or worse, my boyfriend!

Luckily, the shabby dog and I negotiated the blizzard and made it to the main road where my imagined car thief became an instant hero, and I was able to carry on to my destination feeling positive!

I arrived at the meeting and the room was toasty, hot drinks offered, everyone really friendly and I was pumped to be in such a supportive team; then someone started asking about my family. I proudly explained about my five-month-old daughter who I had left at home to come and start my career… except I didn't explain that my five month old was exclusively breastfed and talking about her made my body have an instant reaction. I can only compare the throbbing and urgent need I felt to be away from people to the hulk during his transition!

I quickly made it to the loo where my top was soaking wet and boobs almost at my chin! What could I do? I didn't know anyone in the meeting to text them, I didn't have my bag with my car keys to check for extra clothes in my car, there was no hand dryer, only hand towels available! The venue we were in was a hotel which served food (those were the days!), so I went back to the meeting room holding a hard A4 menu over my chest to hide my predicament as I discreetly put my thick winter coat back on to cover up. After four or five more hours wearing my coat and nearly passing out with the heat, I felt I had earned my 'NQT first day' badge!

Tamsin Nellist
Head of Infants/Foundation Phase Manager

Too Much, Too Young... by Audrey Pantelis

I started teaching as an unqualified teacher in 1991. I was fresh out of university and was a Year 10 form tutor. I had been absent from school the previous day and had noticed that the register had not been taken. I wasn't sure what the procedure was, so I went to the main school office. There was a queue of people ahead of me, so I took my place and waited patiently.

When I was just about to ask about the register and the missing attendance mark, the main receptionist glanced at me and said:
'Just leave it there.'
'Sorry?' I said.
Impatiently:
'You're bringing the register back after your form tutor has taken it? Just leave it there!'
'I am the form tutor.'
Silence.
'Oh – oh ok. How can I help?'

At the time, I was livid that I was not taken seriously as a professional teacher. Nearly thirty years on from that incident – I laugh!!!!

Audrey Pantelis
Director - Talespin Consultancy Ltd (@Audiekins)

It's All in a Week... by Debbie Rainer

Monday

Standing back to admire the large tree branch my husband has cantilevered from the ceiling and attached to piping, I congratulate myself. As a mature NQT attending induction day alongside three university leavers, I had shifted uncomfortably as the head spoke about the difference we would make with our youth, vitality and initiative. My youth had flown, vitality was debatable but no one could deny my initiative. The 'changing with the seasons' book corner would look fabulous once the children hung their autumn leaf book reviews.

Tuesday

My Year 3 class like to be helpful. 'Miss...' 'Just a minute,' I reply, 'let me finish writing.' 'Miss...' 'Please be patient, I'm doing the learning objective.' 'Miss!' 'Not much longer, just finishing off the success criteria.' 'Miss!!!' 'OK Brett, what was it you wanted to say?' 'That's a permanent marker.'

Wednesday

Andrew is an anxious child but the whole class impress me with their deliberate ignoring skills. Not one of us bats an eyelid when he arrives late and crawls the length of the classroom to his desk like a tortoise, covered by his coat. It is not so easy to ignore the school business manager who arrives soon after, clipboard in hand. She spends far too long in the book corner.

Thursday

Whilst on break duty, half my class run over in a panic, they've seen a headless gunman on the other side of the hedge! The deputy headteacher takes their concerns very seriously and springs into action, returning at a sprint to update. Spotting a small child in his path, the whole playground collectively gasps as he leaps aside, saving himself from injury with an impressive forward roll before nonchalantly standing to brush himself down. Turns out the culprit was an old man bending to weed his garden, rake still in hand.

Friday

A team of us have decided to perform a dance routine to 'Fame' for the talent show, up to now we have discussed pink tutus, leg warmers and fluorescent head bands. Today we move onto choreography, and I jump up to demonstrate the final move, flinging my arms out and almost hitting a colleague who has arrived at the staffroom with good news. My book corner has passed the risk assessment.

Debbie Rainer
NQT in Slough 2004

The Secret by David Rushby

It was a big, complicated, diverse, interesting and joyous school. Working in Hackney, East London was the most productive and life changing place for me to begin to learn how to be a teacher and to grow as a person. Only now do I truly understand the significance of this environment and the sustained and often subconscious effect that it would have on my career.

My Year 2 class represented the blueprint for our future. I had children from all over the world sitting in front of me, and it would be my responsibility to ensure that they could learn together. However, there was no doubt that the learning would be entirely mutual, and that every day would bring new insights that would shape my view of our society. After play, we would have our snack time. We sat together in a circle and talked casually. It was unstructured, fun and important. This time together helped to create our own precious culture, that would grease the wheels for every other success.

Small, slim and serious, and often carrying a scowl, I noticed one of my boys disappearing to his tray after we had finished our fruit each day. This young man was a quiet, Nigerian boy who spent most of his time observing others and with a facial expression that told me that he was always working things out. After the children went home, I considered having a look in his tray, but thought that it would be best to ask him personally the next day. The following day, after fruit, he once again crept to one side, towards his tray. At lunch time, as the children left for play, I asked him for a moment of his time and shared carefully what I had observed. He looked at me with some intensity, uncertain of what to do, and then he went to his tray. He put his hand inside and gathered the contents. He then stood before me and uncurled his hand. There on his palm was a collection of apple pips, about twenty or so. He paused and then told me that he was going to grow his own apples and that he didn't want anyone else to know. When he stated this, he did so as though this was all there could be to being self-sufficient. Almost as though no one else had spotted this opportunity. And I don't think that any of us had.

This situation represented everything about where he had come from, where and how he lived and what he thought was important. I learned on that day, and through the following days, about the simplicity of how children think and that maybe the most valuable ideas are not the ones that are confined to the National Curriculum.

David Rushby
Director of Nautilus Education

Safeguarding and My NQT Year by Jen Reynolds

I started teaching in an inner-city school in Liverpool in 1990. Every morning a teacher had the task of blowing the whistle in the yard full of pupils and parents, whereupon the pupils would line up in their classes and then the teacher would commence sending each line off in an orderly fashion to their classrooms. As an NQT, I dreaded my turn. There was the whole school running riot in the echoing yard and the parents observing a desperate attempt to establish silence and to make their voice heard.

One particular morning, I was thrilled to have appeared to have established enough of a semblance of order and calm to begin to send off the classes, as for once the yard was silent. However, before I could send the first class – and with every pupils' eyes upon me – a mother approached me and said:
'Please can I give Alice in Class 5 a message?'
'Of course,' I replied, smiling.

At which point, all eyes followed the mother who proceeded to stoop down into Alice's face, point a wagging finger and shriek:

'And you, you f***ing little b*tch, if you don't pack in slagging off our Toni, I'm going to deck yer...'

From that day, I worked hard to know the community and parent body of schools I worked with, in order to protect the children better from such assaults.

Jen Reynolds
Primary English Advisor

Adventures in Teacherland by Stephen Rogers

Teaching is a job like no other. As you begin your career, you remember all the training you've had and knowledge gained, you visualise how you will be the one to revolutionise teaching as we know it. Then you get your own class and feel like Alice falling down the rabbit hole! Down into a strange new land where what you thought you knew is turned on its head and every day is different.

It is exciting. It is scary. And that is all part of the journey.

I began my career teaching Year 1, at a challenging school in South London. I had the thrill and terror of actually being responsible for these 30 tiny minds! Who left me in charge? Are they of sound mind?! My first year was a rollercoaster of highs and lows, mistakes, successes and plenty of learning. You will laugh. You will cry. But you will be stronger than ever by the end of it. I taught Year 1 for three years, but still was not sure if teaching was right for me. There was a saying around the school:
'If you can teach here, you can teach anywhere.'

So, I decided to test that theory, and took a job at an international school in Bangkok! Here is where I really fell in love with teaching. This new start was what I needed; I learned new skills, found new approaches and gained confidence. Never underestimate the impact of changing school; every school really is different and no matter how your first year goes, there is much to be said for learning and growing from many settings.

The following year, I was back in London, Notting Hill, learning again from a new, diverse team, with fresh ideas to absorb. Those first five years shaped me as a professional and helped me to actively decide upon the teacher I wanted to become.

Ultimately, teaching is what you make of it. And now, 19 years in, every week presents a new challenge; you never stop learning and it will always be interesting. There are still plenty of days where I feel like I'm a guest at the Mad Hatter's tea party!

You are in the early stages of a crazy, demanding but rewarding journey. Stay positive, watch and copy those teachers you admire. Work hard and be authentic, then you will find your wonderland.

Stephen Rogers
Class Teacher/Co-ordinator

A Lesson Learned! by Terry Ross

In my second year of teaching, I learned a lesson which has stayed with me and I still well up thinking about it. A child joined our school mid-term. He was behind the rest of the class and rarely completed homework (which at the time I was led to believe was very important). I asked his mum in for a meeting – ready to read the riot act that this was not good enough. Mum took the wind out of my sails in three sentences.

Opener: 'Isn't he doing so well? He's reading better than me now.'

Followed by: 'This means I can't help him so please give him homework at the weekend 'cause my mum can read.'

And then: 'Can you help me? Please make sure he uses his dinner ticket for a hot lunch and not a sandwich because we don't have a cooker at home.'

I had no idea the situation some of the children were living in. That meeting changed me and my approach.

Terry Ross
Deputy Principal, Malaysia

Conclusions

We All Learned from Teachers...

It is only right and proper that practising professionals from a diverse range of settings should have had the last say in this book of tips for early career and returning teachers. I have enjoyed every one of their stories – some very funny and some quite stressful – and am so grateful to them for their contributions.

When I first read these contributions as they trickled into my emails – thanks to Twitter – I was struck by the common threads and the connections. There are over fifty years in difference between the youngest and the oldest educators featured in this publication, and yet so many experiences and emotions are similar.

Teaching is a challenging but highly rewarding career full of moments of great hilarity and moments of stress, but these case studies confirm that we all started from a similar point and we all travelled a similar journey. And we all reached this moment in time, having survived the early years spent in the profession and now are filled with a great joy for pupils, schools and the world of education. We all survived, and we all made it!

Use your networks, your mentors, your friends and your social media to broaden your experience and strategies, listen, watch and reflect and who knows – in fifty years you too may be writing about your early experiences in this great profession.

And remember, all the leaders in all the professions and businesses in the world have one thing in common – they all learned from teachers!

APPENDIX 1

Top Tips

As a handy reference, we have collated all of the top tips from throughout the book.

Chapter 1 – My Top Tips for Starting a New Post

- Remember that everyone struggles in some areas at the beginning, persevere – it will all come right in the end.
- Keep calm or at least fake calmness!
- Praise those children who work hard and behave, and ignore those who don't – unless there is danger!
- Ask for help if no one has offered it.
- Accept all the help you can get and listen to your mentor and others.
- Make friends and ask them for advice when you need it.
- Buy a couple of appropriate professional outfits and a change of shirts/tops to accompany them – dress to feel good about yourself.
- Consider your journey to school before accepting a post. Many new teachers need to accept the first job they are offered, but you still need to take care of yourself and – if you can afford it – a small car is still the best means if public transport is too challenging. After a few weeks, you will probably be able to agree a car share with another member of staff for the environment's sake.

Chapter 2 – My Top Tips for Radical Phase or School Moves

- Consider carefully what it is you want to achieve and how best you might do that.
- Talk to friends and colleagues in the profession.
- Research the age you will be teaching.
- Research (discreetly) the school you are applying to.
- Ask (politely) if you can visit the school to be shown round before interview.
- Smile at everyone you meet, but also show serious intent and interest through questions.
- Watch the children, how they behave, how they respond to each other and adults.
- Watch the teachers, how they interact with the children, how they articulate.
- Study wall displays (if time) – they represent creativity, achievement and variety.
- Study your journey, will it be too stressful?

Chapter 3 – My First Five Years as a Teacher by Kirstie Pilmer

Top Tips for Initial Training

- Don't just rely on the training you are being given. Go out and improve yourself. Go on Twitter and immerse yourself in EduTwitter. Look for good practice and teaching ideas by doing lots of reading and talking to other teachers.
- If you get the choice of school, look carefully at their most recent Ofsted inspection. Just because a school is RI, it doesn't mean that you shouldn't go for it, but it will give you a good idea where it is currently on the continuum of improvement.
- Ask for the training you want. There's lots of good training online which is very cheap.

- Don't be afraid to tell your training provider you're not happy with the school if you feel like you are not getting the attention you deserve and need.

Top Tips for Instructing Pupils

- When asking a child to do something, give very short and clear instructions.
- Never assume they know what you mean.
- Try to never show you are shocked by anything.

Top Tips for Settling into a Class

- Ask for help. If you know something hasn't gone well, ask how you could have improved it, or how others would have done it differently.
- Have the confidence to be open and honest about your lessons.
- Laugh about your mistakes. Everyone makes them and they can be quite humorous when you look back on them.

Top Tips for Attending Interviews

- Be prepared for the interview: take folders with pictures of displays, reports from training, lesson observations (the good ones).
- Be prepared for your lesson: have any printed material in wallets so you can quickly pass them around the tables, take any practical equipment with you, think of some good activities the children can be doing whilst you are setting up, like counting.
- Question the children to get a good grasp on what they can already do so you can differentiate the rest of the lesson accordingly.
- Ring the school before hand to ask for abilities, topics studied, SEND.
- Fake it in the classroom. Be the most confident person you can be.
- If possible, reflect on the lesson with someone who has observed you. This shows that you want to improve and be a better teacher.

Top Tips for Maturing as a Teacher

- Prioritise: you can't do everything, so make sure you do the important jobs first. If you don't change a display for half a term, does it really matter?
- If you are not sure which jobs to prioritise, ask someone with more experience.
- Always ask yourself why. If you don't think it's important, then don't do it.
- Enjoy what you do. If you are enthusiastic about what you are teaching, then the children will be enthusiastic about learning.
- Talk to your colleagues (this is something I found really tough); ask them for advice and have a cup of tea and talk about your problems.

Chapter 4 – My Top Tips for Returning to Teaching

- Don't return to work unless you are fully recovered from whatever caused your absence.
- Don't return to work unless you are in the right frame of mind – or are confident you can fake it!
- Seek people out, make connections, smile and make eye contact.
- Smile and say 'good morning' to people.
- Ask for advice or help if you need it.
- If you have to, 'fake it to make it'.

Chapter 5 – My Top Tips for Establishing a Persona as a Teacher

- Be aware of the image you are portraying.
- Watch the demeanour of those you admire as they move around the school and interact with others.
- Adopt and adapt strategies you admire.
- Move with confidence, head held high.
- Greet people as you pass.
- Make eye contact.
- Smile.
- If you fake it well it will become real.

Chapter 6 – My Top Tips for Incentives and Rewards

- Don't be afraid to use them.
- Don't promise something you are not going to fulfil.
- Make pupils believe in themselves and their abilities.
- Give pupils confidence and a thirst for learning.
- Use the carrot not the stick.
- Praise more often than you criticise.
- Make learning enjoyable and rewarding.
- Empower pupils with choice and time management as a powerful reward.

Chapter 7 – My Top Tips for Aspiring to Be Inspiring

- Improve your subject knowledge so that you can divert and follow the lead of the class when appropriate.
- Be flexible and listen to the class.
- Arouse passion in yourself to arouse passion in your pupils.
- Convey excitement and joy in the learning.
- Use humour consciously and effectively.
- Enrich your teaching with anecdotes when appropriate.
- Slip in the unexpected.
- Believe in your pupils and trust them.

Chapter 8 – My Top Tips for Planning

- Always plan at least one more activity than you think time allows, you can always use it the next day but there is nothing worse than a lesson finishing early and you having nothing 'up your sleeve'.
- Don't write more than you need to teach the lesson and to respond to the children's understanding and ideas.
- Always make sure you know more about the subject than you expect the children to learn so that you can be responsive to questions or comments.
- Always be prepared to respond to the children's interest in the subject, to go 'off plan' if it is appropriate and do not 'fob them off' and say, 'No, we are learning about this.'
- Always have short time fillers available if needed.
- Consider trying short integrated periods when the time is right.

Chapter 9 – My Top Tips for Differentiation

- Try different methods with a child to see which appear to work best for them.
- Try not to rely on yourself for support to a child for more than a few minutes.
- Do not just give extra work to the most able child but rather plan in additional challenge.
- Always ask yourself if any work set is just a 'holding' activity.
- Plan access to the learning for the child who does not yet fully understand English, mainly through seating with another speaker of the same first language, through key word translation and through use of pictures and mime.
- Use translation sites on the internet to find key words.

Chapter 10 – My Top Tips for Classroom Organisation

- Give every child a dedicated seat or let them choose their own and don't move them unless there are concerns about behaviour.
- Ensure all children can see the whiteboard at all times, without having to turn round.
- Make the classroom environment a pleasant and attractive place to be.
- Keep cupboard tops clean and tidy.
- Invest time and patience in learning to make displays of the highest quality possible.

Chapter 11 – My Top Tips for Managing Behaviour

- Make your boundaries clear from the start.
- Don't ignore first minor infringements.
- Deal with first slips discreetly but firmly.
- Never humiliate children.
- Agree a short set of class rules and display them clearly at the front of the room.
- Ensure all know and understand the rules.
- Point to the relevant rule if raising an issue.
- Praise good behaviour constantly.
- Praise the more difficult child whenever possible and ensure they feel part of the 'family'.
- Remember, there are often stressful circumstances in a child's life if their behaviour is often poor.
- Build a feeling of belonging to something special – a feeling of 'family'.

Chapter 12 – My Top Tips for Discussion and Debate

- Develop a culture of respect and good manners.
- Have clear rules about listening and not talking when someone else is.
- Proactively teach dialogic phrases for opening sentences.
- Give a paddle or a card thumbs-up hand for children to indicate they are ready to contribute.
- Always choose interesting topics related to studies or news.
- Praise and encourage.
- Be patient if someone is fumbling and expect the class to be too.

Chapter 13 – My Top Tips for Marking and Assessment

- Study the standards achieved by children of the age you teach.
- Marking and feedback are both important, although all work may not need to be marked (especially not always in the foundation subjects) if formative assessment has been achieved in other ways. Remember, it is valued by children – so do it with pride.
- Ask pupils to discuss your marking and comments in pairs.
- Listen to children and watch them work.
- Diagnose the problem when a child or group constantly make the same errors.

Chapter 14 – My Top Tips for Policy into Practice

- Study the school policies and be sure you are interpreting them as intended.
- Implement school policies to the very best of your ability.
- Do seek help if you have difficulty interpreting or implementing a policy.
- Do consult leadership if you have personal difficulty with underlying principles in a policy.
- Avoid bringing outside agencies into the discussions unless absolutely desperate.
- Avoid involving the governors unless advised to by leadership or – as a last resort – to have a confidential consultation for advice.
- Apply for new jobs if you find you cannot agree with important policies after a reasonable period.
- Establish your personal red lines and ask about them at interview.
- Avoid becoming a moaner/grumbler within school.

Chapter 15 – My Top Tips for Diversity

- Every Child Matters.
- Make every child feel valued and important.
- Seek out the quiet child and build their esteem.
- Seek out the angry child and build their esteem.
- Seek out the isolated child and build their esteem.
- Develop a culture of inclusion where every child does matter and is valued.
- Embrace all the other cultures represented in the school.
- Ensure that, within your teaching, diverse ethnicities and cultures are promoted and celebrated.

APPENDIX 2

Final Thoughts

Teaching was fun and flexible thirty years ago; it is up to us as a profession to make it that way again. We were able to respond to children's needs which promoted their sense of belonging and engagement – **Sara Alston**

The moral of the story is: decide what the key ingredient of your lesson is, what do you actually want the children to learn? Then plan from that, as opposed to putting on a show – **Humaira Batool**

My Reception children were happily playing. The next minute, a huge, rabid looking Alsatian dog launched itself in through the window into the middle of a classroom full of unsuspecting four year olds – **Ginny Bootman**

Little did I realise that the window was unfastened and as I leant back, the window opened and I literally fell backwards straight out – **Alex Caunt**

Miss Warren was firm, fair and friendly. I became her. This became my style of teaching too, until it felt natural to work in this way – **Sharon Day**

Day two of my teaching career, and I found myself and some new colleagues in a pitch-black forest trying to find the place where 60 children from our school were camping – **Joshua Denton-Collins**

'What did the judge say to the dentist? Do you swear to pull the tooth, the whole tooth and nothing but the tooth?' – **Rachel Gregson**

...the officer shouted 'Son, get back! Please go and get your teacher!' The officer refused to believe that I wasn't a pupil! – **Sam Keys**

Do I perform the walk of shame to try and find someone or stay and supervise my new tutor group, who are quickly losing patience? In a desperate act of survival and self-deprecation, I mocked my inauspicious introduction to the group – **Steve Ladd**

The profession needs to find a midway point, with the creativity and freedoms I experienced in my early years counterbalanced by the accountability required today – **Hayley McDonnell**

If you are bored planning a lesson, then the children will be bored taking part in the lesson. If an idea, concept or activity excites you, then it will excite the kids too… – **Katy McCullough**

As I saw my shiny Golf accelerate away, I stood in a snow storm in the middle of nowhere. With no phone reception and a dog on a shabby lead whose name I didn't know, I wondered how I would explain this to my new employer – or worse, my boyfriend! – **Tamsin Nellist**

…the main receptionist glanced at me and said: 'Just leave it there.' 'Sorry?' I said. Impatiently: 'You're bringing the register back after your form tutor has taken it? Just leave it there!' 'I am the form tutor.' Silence. 'Oh – oh ok. How can I help?' – **Audrey Pantelis**

'Miss…' 'Just a minute,' I reply, 'let me finish writing.' 'Miss…' 'Please be patient, I'm doing the learning objective.' 'Miss!' 'Not much longer, just finishing off the success criteria.' 'Miss!!!' 'That's a permanent marker.' – **Debbie Rainer**

My Year 2 class represented the blueprint for our future. I had children from all over the world sitting in front of me, and it would be my responsibility to ensure that they could learn together – **David Rushby**

From that day, I worked hard to know the community and parent body of schools I worked with, in order to protect the children better – **Jen Reynolds**

I began my career teaching Year 1, at a challenging school in South London. I had the thrill and terror of actually being responsible for these 30 tiny minds! Who left me in charge? Are they of sound mind?! – **Stephen Rogers**

I had no idea the situation some of the children were living in. That meeting changed me and my approach – **Terry Ross**